INDUSTRIAL PSYCHOLOGY

Table of Contents

CHAPTER 1: INTRODUCTION

Industrial Psychology is a scientific study of employees, workplaces, organizations and organizational behavior. Industrial psychology is also known as work psychology, organizational psychology. An Industrial psychologist contributes by improving the workplaces, satisfaction and motivation levels of the employees, and helping the overall productivity of the organization.

The specialty of industrial psychology is characterized by the scientific study of human behavior in organizations and the work place. The specialty focuses on deriving principles of individual, group and organizational behavior and applying this knowledge to the solution of problems at work.

Industrial psychology is a relatively young field. The industrial aspect focuses on improving, evaluating, and predicting job performance, while the organizational aspect focuses on how organizations impact and interact with individuals.

HISTORY OF INDUSTRIAL PSYCHOLOGY

A Brief Overview

Industrial-Organizational psychology has only been in existence for about the last century. It was primarily an outgrowth of the Industrial Revolution. When factories and assembly lines began coming into existence, the people who ran the factories wanted to try to get as much money as possible out of their workers. The first industrial psychologists weren't as interested in employees being satisfied and happy as they were about making sure that the jobs were designed to be as efficient and streamlined as possible. A landmark study of this time period involved a study to make trolley operators be as productive as possible, and another involved how best to design a coal shovel to increase production.

The Hawthorne Effect

In one of the early studies (1924-1932) conducted by I-O psychologist Harry Landsberger, a factory was interested in seeing how changing work conditions would affect employee output. For example, Landsberger wanted to see how low the lighting could be and still maintain optimal productivity. While conducting these experiments, the results weren't at all what he expected. It appeared that no matter what he did, the employees improved their production speed, even if he only gave them low candlelight to work by. After post-analysis, Landsberger discovered that the employees were performing better because there were people around them wearing white coats, carrying clipboards, interested in what they were doing. Thus, work conditions had been trumped by employee feelings about someone being interested in what they were doing.

The Rise of Testing

Any business that has had profits increased by some sort of testing or interview process owes its success to how World War I and II occurred. Because both of these conflicts occurred without the United States being prepared for them, huge numbers of incoming soldiers needed to be placed in jobs they were best suited for as quickly as possible. Psychologists used their knowledge of testing to sort people into different jobs based on brief, massed assessments and did so with great accuracy. When these psychologists returned from the wars, they brought their knowledge home with them and applied their new knowledge of selections to businesses. What we see today in almost every aspect of testing for selections is an outgrowth of this era in history.

Human Capital Becomes Important

Studies like Landsberger's and the new knowledge of how to select employees started to change industrial psychology. This also began to cause industrial psychologists and businesses to think of employees as resources to be managed and retained, instead of thinking about them as tools that could be replaced if they weren't performing properly. The shift wasn't necessarily an ethical change where businesses suddenly acted out of an interest in humanism instead of profits. This shift was primarily because of the evidence that industrial psychologists provided, showing that employee retention and management was more profitable. All of these changes have led to where industrial psychology and business have come to be today.

APPLICATIONS/USES OF INDUSTRIAL PSYCHOLOGY

Since Industrial Psychology is the study of people at work and is concerned with the entire spectrum of human, its scope is the entire process of management dealing with people at work.

There is hardly a field in industry where human understanding is not required; there is hardly a problem in industry and business where human aspect is not involved and hence there is hardly an area in which industrial psychology cannot play its role. Industrial psychology is a useful aid to the efficient management of people at work. The principles and techniques of industrial psychology may be applied to the following areas of management:

1) Recruitment—Appropriate matching of job requirement with the employee's abilities lead to reduction in the cost of hiring, supervision and production. Accurate job analysis, standardized application forms, scientific screening of applications, use of psychological tests for vocational fitness, final overall rating and continuous review and check-up of the entire programme are some of the spheres where the psychologist can make an important contribution several psychological tests may be developed for the proper screening of the people. In this way, psychology may help in recruiting the right man to the right job.

2) Selection and Placement-Right man should be selected for the right job and industrial psychology helps in this effort also. It develops various devices such as interviews and psychological tests in order to achieve the objective of the selection. It also helps the placement of workers at different jobs scientific assignment of job is possible only with the help of industrial psychology.

3) Executive Development and Training—a psychologist by studying and investigating managerial problems like delegation, communication and supervision vitalizes the already practiced managerial psychology. Individual differences can well be measured by psychological study of the people for training purposes. Continuous and effective use of the capabilities of workers necessitates training of the workers and supervisors. Psychology determines what type of training should be given to the workers.

4) Promotional Schemes—Why should a man be promoted or transferred or demoted or discharged. These employment situations should be based on abilities, usefulness and seniority. Performance appraisal is one of the psychological techniques to recognize the peoples' ability mere seniority should not be the guiding principle for promotions.

5) Motivation—the psychologists assume that the causes of different types of human behaviour in industry and business are the needs or the motives that drive an individual to behave in a particular way. Industrial psychology problems into behaviour of people at work to determine the conditions in which an individual or people at work to determine the conditions in which an individual feels motivated and is willing to work whole-heartedly to maximize the productivity. Industrial psychology has identified the financial and non-financial incentives which are used by the management to motivate the personnel.

6) Attitude and morale—The psychologists have established the relationship between the attitudes of the employees and their performance. Psychological studies outline the major factors favorable or detrimental to good morale and give some class as to the steps which can be taken to give further understanding of needs, perceptions, satisfaction and motivation of people in relation to their working situations.

7) Wages and salary administration-The wage rates in the industry should be fixed on some suitable and scientific formula. The psychologists have developed the techniques of job evaluation, merit-rating and job analysis as basis for rational wage and salary structure. Job evaluation and merit-rating are the techniques which evaluate the worth of the job and of the man respectively. Merit-ratings technique evaluates the men while the job analysis determines the job description and worth of the job.

8) Human relations—Human relations may briefly be described as the relations or contacts among individuals in an organisation and the group behaviour that emerges from these relations. The modern industrial psychologists treated people in industry as human being and have made significant contribution to industrial management by developing concepts and techniques of effective leadership. They suggest the possible ways and means to solve the industrial strife.

9) Human engineering-It is designing and laying out equipment in order to get the greatest efficiency of man-machine system. The industrial psychologists working in human engineering provides data on which management can decide to improve the design and the product for the comfort and to increase the sale to the satisfaction of customers. It also helps in reducing machine breakdowns, wastage of raw materials and training time to workers, to minimize accidents and introduce better performance and job satisfaction. Industrial psychology has humanized the management and opened the way to a much fuller utilisation of the human factor in industry.

10) Accident prevention—the psychological studies show that 98% of the accidents in industry are preventable. It means personal or psychological factors play an important role in any programme of accident prevention. Monotony and fatigue studies help in minimizing the accidents. Psychologists have made the contribution of signals to the development of safety programme and the preservation of human factor in industry.

SCOPES OF INDUSTRIAL PSYCHOLOGY

1. Economic, Social and Psychological Aspect of the Industry

Industrial psychology deals with human behavior in the entire industrial environment. Consequently, it studies the economic, social and psychological aspects of human behaviour. In the modern age most of economic factors have some psychological influence. The various factors in communal life of workers living in industrial environment also influence the psychology of the worker. Industrial psychology studies these factors.

2. Study of the Physical Aspect of Work Environment

In an industry the worker is greatly influenced by the working conditions. If the conditions are well, the worker feels satisfied and remains healthy while on the other hand if the conditions are got good the workers become dissatisfied. Industrial psychology deals with the physical working conditions.

3. Principles of Human Relationships

Irrespective of the automation introduced in industries, the human element cannot be eliminated Even most efficient machine needs an engineer to run it, and because the engineer is a human being the most importance of the psychological element in the running of the factory cannot be ignored. The efficiency of the human being will depend very much upon the nature of his relations with the management.

In the previous century most industrialists behaved like autocrats and considered the workers as nothing more than tools. But in that period the efficiency level was not very high.

It has been seer that an industrialist can achieve a higher rate of production if he behaves sympathetically with his employees. An industrialist who cannot maintain good relations with his workers does not succeed for long time. Industrial psychology tries at discover principles for improving human relationships in an industrial environment.

4. Study of Aptitudes and Motives- why people behave the way they do

As in any other circumstances, human behaviour in the industrial environment is influenced and formed by attitudes and aims. Behaviour changes with the changes in stimuli. Hence it is very important to study the rules pertaining to correct attitudes and aims.

Industrial psychology pursues this kind of study. An important example of study of this kind is the study conducted by Hawthorne Works Western Electric Company into the effect of the attitudes of workers upon production. This study is known as the Hawthorne Study.

5. Study of Principles of Mental Health (work conditions can affect health of employees)

Today all intelligent people realize the importance of maintaining the proper health of workers. The workers mental health is influenced by working conditions and by the attitude of other people towards him. Industrial psychology not only studies the factors influencing the mental health of industrial works but also tries to discover principles for maintaining their mental health. Industrial "psychology also gives suggestions for improving the mental health of those who are suffering from mental disease or are otherwise unbalanced.

6. Study of Human Relation-study of human behaviour

Industrial psychology is the study or human behaviour in an industrial context. Being a branch of psychology, industrial psychology is particularly concerned with the observation and study, of human relations to reach conclusion through experiment and other studies. On the basis of these conclusions it tries to discover general principles which can be used to improve social relations between the workers and the management.

CONCEPTS OF THE PERSON IN WORK PSYCHOLOGY

Psychology Concepts for Improving Employee Motivation

The following concepts are some of the more important theories in motivational psychology in terms of workplace behavior:

- **Intrinsic Motivation**

What drives action? Those who have a desire to effectively perform behaviors for their own sake are said to have intrinsic motivation. Reading a psychology article indicates that you have intrinsic motivation towards understanding human nature. Same rule applies in the workplace. Those workers who love being at work and will do anything it takes for the company to flourish are most of the time intrinsically motivated. Put in other words, *they have a passion to succeed.*

- **Extrinsic Motivation**

Commissions, sales incentives and social praise are well-known motivators. The psychological concept is extrinsic motivation. These rewards can be extremely powerful when looking to motivate your staff to go above and beyond their current comfort zone of productivity.

- **Over justification Effect**

The over justification effect occurs when someone naturally has a passion (intrinsic motivation) to see something through, but is offered a reward for its completion, thus rendering them less effective. For instance, if an employee loves writing on the corporate blog but the management decide to financially compensate them for each post. There is a chance they will find the writing less enjoyable. Since they have to be bribed into writing, then the task must not be worth doing for its own sake.

- **Positive Reinforcement**

Strengthening or diminishing certain employee behaviors is extremely important when developing a highly effective team. This can be achieved with a basic understanding of operant conditioning. Essentially, the concept describes how the effects of **praise and reward** can be used to refine behavior. While this can be seen throughout life, you can apply the concept when motivating your workforce.

For instance, praising one of your employees (in front of their peers is best) after they made a nice improvement in their numbers during the previous week will result in a greater urge to repeat, or top, those numbers in hopes of further praise. A few examples of positive reinforcements in the workplace are social praise in public, sales incentives & bonuses as well as creative rewards such as early departure from work, casual dress days and in-office game/personal time.

- **Shaping**

After a while, positive reinforcement will become less effective as they will become accustomed to the praise. Withholding the reward unless performance is continually improved upon will help shape the productivity. To illustrate this concept, imagine a bookkeeper that has been openly rewarded for getting the expenses entered in 8 hours. But you have found that the 8-hour timeframe has become the norm. If you feel the job can be done in 5 hours you must praise their performance only as the timeframe improves and ignore slower results.

- **Achievement Motivation Theory**

The desire to achieve the absolute best results possible is an amazing trait to find in coworkers. Those who strive to achieve share these three major characteristics:

1. They favor a work environment in which they are able to assume responsibility for solving problems.
2. They tend to take calculated risks and to set moderate, attainable goals.
3. They need continuing recognition and feedback about their progress so that they know how well they are doing.

Furthermore, these high achievers have been found to carry two different goals – mastery and performance. Which means that as a leader you must recognize what makes these workers tick? The high achievers who strive for mastery of tasks are driven by developing themselves internally and are rewarded by becoming increasingly skilled. Performance based achievers need to be the best. They find satisfaction by completing their duties better than their coworkers.

- **Needs Hierarchy Theory**

Sometimes called Maslow's Hierarchy of Needs, the concept illustrates human needs, arranged in order of importance. The lower needs on this pyramid must be fulfilled before one can achieve the next higher level:

Abraham Maslow's Hierachy of Needs

This chart is important for entrepreneurs and leaders to understand. For example, if an employee is lacking self-esteem or self-fulfillment in their life, there is little chance of them becoming an extremely remarkable addition to your team. You must recognize and create solutions for your staff to become truly satisfied in their life before you can achieve the results you desire.

- **Motivator-Hygiene Theory**

Also called the Two-Factor Theory, the Motivator-Hygiene Theory isn't backed by a lot of supporting data in the psychology/research world. But it has transformed many organizations in terms of employee motivation. The concept is based on the suggestion that an employee has two needs:

1. **Motivator Needs** – These produce job satisfaction and are considered higher needs. They can be satisfied by providing stimulating, challenging and absorbing work. Meeting these demands will result in job satisfaction. *However, the lack of a challenging job will not create job dissatisfaction.*

2. **Hygiene Needs** – These produce job dissatisfaction and are considered lower needs. A few examples of these needs are a company policy, working conditions, wages paid and other external factors that can directly affect a worker such as their supervisor. Meeting these needs does not result in job satisfaction but rather prevents job dissatisfaction.

The take away from this concept is that as you oversee your organization, it is important to emphasize job enrichment. Put in other words, be sure to maximize the potential of every single employee by consciously recognizing the opportunities to promote satisfaction and demote dissatisfaction in the workplace.

- **Equity Theory**

Ensuring that your employees feel equal amongst their peers is extremely important when creating a motivated workforce. The equity theory describes how workers assess their efforts and outcomes on the job by calculating a "productivity ratio." They then (most likely unconsciously) compare their ratio to the perceived ratios of their coworkers.

Further studies have expanded on this theory by classifying three types of equatorial behaviors:

1. **Benevolent** – These workers feel satisfied when under-rewarded compared to coworkers and feel guilty when equally or over-rewarded.
2. **Equity-Sensitive** – These workers believe everyone should be rewarded fairly. They dislike when they are under-rewarded and guilty when over-rewarded.
3. **Entitled** – These workers feel they should be over-rewarded in comparison to their coworkers and dislike anything less.

The important idea here is that you must keep a careful eye on the workforce's perceptions in regards to pay and rewards.

- **Goal Setting Theory**

The goal setting theory is somewhat common sense but it reinforces the fact that a worker's motivation shares a direct relationship with their goals. This theory was developed by Edward Locke and illustrates that by setting specific and challenging goals for your team motivation will provoke extreme productivity. From profit goals for your sales force to timeframe goals for your research team, your overall business will benefit greatly by implementing this strategy.

- **Valence-Instrumentality-Expectancy (VIE) Theory**

This theory may be one of the most important concepts for motivation – *but is often overlooked by most businesses.* The VIE theory states that people are motivated to perform as expected because of the prospect of personal advancement such as a pay-raise or promotion. Put in other words, workers who aspire for a better status at work will do anything they believe will get them their desired results.

So what does this mean for your business? It conveys the fact you must clearly illustrate what actions you are looking for when it comes to your employee's possible pay-raises, bonuses and promotions.

Conclusion

As a leader, understanding your team's underlying desires and their motivating forces will be essential for your continued success.

INTRODUCTION TO INDIVIDUAL DIFFERENCES

No two persons are born exactly alike; but each differs from the other in natural endowments, one being suited for one occupation and the other for another.

Individual differences are a cornerstone subject area in modern psychology. In many ways, it is the "classic" psychology that the general public refers as the psychological differences between people and their similarities.

Individual difference psychology examines how people are similar and how they differ in their thinking, feeling and behaviour. No two people are alike, yet no two people are unlike. So, in the study of individual differences we strive to understand ways in which people are psychologically similar and particularly what psychological characteristics vary between people.

It is generally assumed that:

- People vary on a range of psychological attributes
- It is possible to measure and study these individual differences
- individual differences are useful for explaining and predicting behaviour and

performance

We can classify people psychologically, according to their intelligence and personality characteristics, for example, with moderate success, however people are complex and much is still left unexplained. There are multiple and often conflicting theories and evidence about individual difference psychology.

Human beings have been aware of individual differences throughout history, e.g.

- Gender differences
- Intelligence differences
- Personality differences

Nature of Individual Differences
It has been observed that if we collect information about people's characteristics from a large sample and examine the pattern of distribution, we find that a large majority of the people fall in the middle range while a small proportion lies in extreme categories. For example, most of the people fall in the category of average height and very few are very tall or very short. This holds true for many more characteristics including intelligence and other psychological attributes.

The fact that people are different from each other is a very common observation. The differences in psychological characteristics are often consistent and form a stable pattern. By 'consistent', we mean that people tend to show regularity in their behaviour and their patterns of behaviour do not change very frequently. This consistency and stability in behaviour is unique to every person. People develop their unique traits/ characteristics and patterns of behaviour due to their genetic make-up and the environment in which they are brought up. Once we know these differences systematically we can utilize the capabilities of people efficiently for their healthy development. Knowing about the specific characteristics of a person is necessary in order to extend support and utilize his or her potential to optimal level.

Individual differences occur due to interaction of *genetic and environmental* factors. We inherit certain characteristics from our parents through genetic codes. The phenotype or the expressed forms of our characteristics depend on contributions of the *socio-cultural environment*. This is the reason why we are not exactly like our parents and our parents not exactly like our grandparents. We do share similarities with our parents in respect of many physical attributes like height, color of eyes, shape of nose etc. We also inherit certain cognitive, emotional and other characteristics from our parents like intellectual competence, love for sport, creativity etc. However, our own characteristics develop largely by the support from the environment which we inhabit. The environment is responsible as how we are reared, the kind of atmosphere at house, whether it is liberal or strict, the type of education that we get, what we learn from people, around us, books, cultural practices, peers, teachers and media All these aspects refer to 'environment' which help in developing our potentials.

By providing models and other opportunities, *environment* helps us develop many traits and skills. Our inheritance alone cannot decide what we become but our environment also contributes to our personalities. One can be born in a very poor family but, with the right education and environment, became a great person, e.g Ben Carson who a world is known neurosurgeon.

Now you know that our genetic codes vary. At the same time, surrounding environment also differs from person to person. It sets limits or defines a range by offering different opportunities. That is why the pattern of development of each of us is different from others. It makes us think why we are similar in certain ways and different in others.

Task: Explain the term 'individual differences

Nature of Personality

We all use the term 'personality' in day-to-day life. In psychology personality is thought as a person's unique and relatively stable behaviour pattern which remains consistent across situations and over a period of time. The term personality has been defined in diverse ways.

Personality is the dynamic organization within the individual of those psychophysical systems that determine his unique adjustment to his environment". Psychologists have approached personality from different perspectives. Each of these perspectives explains some aspects of personality. They include:

- *The trait perspective:*

This tries to describe personality in terms of various traits. Sometimes the traits are grouped into clusters. These clusters are called "types". For instance introversion and extraversion are two types of personality traits.

- *The psychodynamic perspective*

This calls attention to the unconscious needs and conflicts as well as the influence of earlier stages of development on our lives..

- *The socio-cultural perspective*

This highlights the importance of the social and cultural environment. In view of this theory, our personality and behaviour patterns are acquired through interaction with others and adoption of social and cultural norms.

- *The humanistic perspective*

This emphasizes the enormous potential for freedom and growth present in each one of us. It is a view which is optimistic and emphasizes-on positive aspects of life and potentialities.

PERSONALITY TYPES

A b c d personality types:

The Classification of personality types into the four major categories a,b,c and d is one of the very accurate personality type assessments.

However, you might find that you have Type D personality traits but still find that you have some personality traits from another type such as type C. You will also have tons of other personality traits that are not covered at all by a single theory, that's why one personality type theory is certainly insufficient to help you understand yourself well.

Type A personality traits

Type A personalities are competitive, high achievers and have a high sense of time urgency. As a result of these combined traits Type A's are always found to be busy working on their own projects. Type A's felt insecure at one point of their lives and so they decided to fight the insecurity by changing their lives and making achievements as fast as they can.

Type B personality traits

Type B's are the opposite of type A's. They are relaxed, laid back and not easily stressed. While type B can be achievers too still they won't be as competitive as Type A's. Type b can delay work and do it in the last moment, some of them can turn into procrastinators which is something that a type A can never do.

Type C personality traits

Type C personalities love details and can spend a lot of time trying to find out how things work and this makes them very suitable for technical jobs. Type C are not assertive at all and they always suppress their own desires even if there is something that they dislike. The lack of assertiveness results in tremendous **stress** and sometimes in depression. Type Cs are very vulnerable to depression compared to type A and type B.

Type D personality traits

D stands for distressed; Type D's have a negative outlook towards life and are pessimistic. A small event that is not even noticed by type B can ruin type D's day. Type D might become socially withdrawn as a result of fear of rejection even if they like to be around people.

Type D's are famous for suppressing their emotions and this makes them the most vulnerable type to depression. In my book, The ultimate guide to getting over depression i said that one of the famous causes for depression is suppressing your emotions for long periods of time without venting them someway.

Managing Different Personalities - People Management Skills

You will encounter many different types of people during your management career. If you are managing a group of around 20 or less, you really should be able to get a feel for each individual's personality. Even if you manage a group of 100, you should still be able to know the key players personalities. It helps when you know what makes each one of them tick, especially when communicating one-on-one. When dealing with different personalities, be tolerant of styles different from your own. Always try to adapt to their personality to get your point across, or to get more out of them.

You can't use a cookie cutter approach with every employee. In most cases, you will need to change your communication approach with each individual. For example, you will not get your point across if you're too direct and data oriented with a touchy-feely kind of person. In the same token, you would not want to be too touchy-feely with a no-nonsense type of person. This is also important when delegating any projects to individuals or as small teams. If a person or team is too analytical, there will be little creativity. If a person or team is too sensitive, fewer decisions will be confidently made. Here are some ways to deal with different personality traits:

- The **"Considerate"** are nice, calm, and like to think things through. They usually have an optimistic "glass half-full" point of view. They are agreeable, but might take a bit longer than others to get the work done. They might need some help in making decisions. The good news is usually the work is more complete with fewer errors. Let them know calmly, yet directly, what you need from them. However, also spend some time to talk about family and other non-work related topics. This would be a good person to do long-term detailed oriented type of projects. Give a lot of encouragement and praise to get the most out of this type of personality.

- The **"Aggressive"** likes to take control and do things quickly. They are not afraid to make decisions. They are usually good at what they do, and know it. Just make sure they do not try and control you. They can produce a lot of good work for you, but every once and a while you need to make sure they know whose boss. Be direct, straightforward, and use a no-nonsense approach to business. This would be a good person to use to put out any fires that need immediate attention. Make sure you give this person a lot of praise when praise is due. If you don't, they will be upset.

- The **"Analyst"** will always try to find flaws in the system. They will also play devil's advocate. If you say, "Do this," they will say, "why don't we do it like that?" Sometimes it's a good thing because there might indeed be a better solution, but most of the time it's just someone being too critical. They tend to procrastinate when making decisions. Listen to what they have to say, but if you feel it is going nowhere, take their suggestions and move quickly onto the next subject. This would be a good person to give projects like finding possible trouble producing trends that requires deep analytical investigation. This is more of a "just the facts" type of person. Don't waste either of your time to chat about subjects of little importance.

- The **"Sensitive"** takes any type of confrontation too personally. They do as they are told, but do not like making decisions. They are usually very nice and pleasant but their feelings get hurt too easily. Try not to be too direct with this type of personality. Use an encouraging type of approach when dealing with any performance related issues. This would be a good person to give projects that are more "touchy-feely."

- The **"Talkative"** tend to be more feelings oriented and will show more emotion, whether positive or negative. They have a strong interest about people and are usually the "social butterfly" of the department. They usually like making decisions but want conformation just in case. Try using a lightened-up approach and some humor to get your point across to this type of personality. This would be a good person to help plan social events or any projects that require some animated personality.

- The **"Brainiac"** will use knowledge and sarcasm to get what they want. They will try and dance around the basic topic. They will also dance around making any type of decision. Make sure you keep this person on track as they can lose focus on the task at hand very easily. If needed, make them repeat themselves in terms everyone can understand. This would be a good person to give the projects that are more "data-oriented."

- The **"Quiet"** is one who very rarely talks at meetings, seems to have low self-esteem, and is continually sub-conscious of their actions. Not only should you try to bring this person out of their shell, they just might have some brilliant ideas that you can incorporate. There can be power in the quiet person as they might be the ones with the most compelling ideas. We tend to give our attention to the commanding personalities and ignore the quiet and soft-spoken. On the contrary, the quiet people are the ones you need to seek out.

- The **"Results-Driven"** tend to focus solely on targeted metrics but sometimes lose focus on the big picture. They feel like they are doing a great job because of meeting an important goal, however, they are doing a poor job on another aspect of the job. You need to get your point across by being direct. You have to stress the importance of the big picture and to use common sense. For example, this is the type of person who will stop troubleshooting a problem, even if they are close to fixing it, because they went over the average call handle time. This person is usually more suited for simple straightforward tasks that do not require thinking outside of the box.

- The **"Loner"** just wants to do the job and not get involved with company picnics, break room conversations, or any non-work related subjects. They do not like any interaction with fellow employees. You should talk to them about the importance and reasoning of the team approach. It is to their benefit if the team exceeds, not only for job security, but also for any possible rewards you have in place. With open and honest communication, you should be able to get them to understand and work as a team member. This does not mean they have to be everyone's best friend; they just need to be supportive and reliable. The problem with a person who does not want to be part of a team usually ends up not fully understanding the expectations of the group, and will have the type of excuse like, "Nobody told me…" or "I did not know I was supposed to do that…" etc. This person might be a diamond in the rough and if they just do not fit in to the current team, see if there is another position that would be better suited for them. This might look like you are rewarding someone because of a personality issue, so be careful how you handle this as it could create conflict amongst your team. You, and most likely HR, will have to determine the outcome of such a move. Still continue to try to get this person out of their shell, and try to give them projects that do not demand a team effort.

- The **"Overly-Confident"** feels like they know everything and can do no wrong. Sometimes they act confident even when they don't know what they're doing. You need to get your point across by being very direct. You might want to humble this person every now and then. Make them repeat exactly what it is they are supposed to be doing. Give them projects that can easily be tracked to make sure they are not headed in the wrong direction.

- The **"Curmudgeon"** thinks of everyone but them self as incompetent, and does not take supervision well. They tend to be grumpy and sarcastic. They have a pessimistic "glass is half-empty" point of view. You do not want to approach this type of person with your tail between your legs. State the facts and let them know exactly what is expected of them. Use a matter of fact approach and try to give them projects that do not demand too much creativity or touchy-feely.

- The **"Mean-Spirited"** makes it known that they are not happy with work or the people around them. In many cases it is due to problems that are not work related. If you feel that it is affecting employee morale, you should talk to this person and make sure they understand that you need a department that works in harmony. That the goal is to a have everyone work in a pleasant atmosphere in which there are no personality conflicts.

- The **"Bad Attitude"** is a major problem. You need to let this person know that their attitude is affecting morale and is unacceptable.

How to Successfully Work With Different Personalities

Likeability is a key factor to workplace success. If personality conflicts occur in the office, productivity slows and targets are missed. Here are five ways to deal with different personality types:

1. *Give a feedback sandwich.* You may like speaking your mind, but others may not like to hear it. Most workers have a tough time receiving negative feedback, even when it's from someone they know, like, and admire. To ease the situation, try implementing a feedback sandwich. Start on a positive note ("I really like the work you've been completing"), continue with the potentially

abrasive feedback ("but would love to see you meet deadlines"), and then end on another positive note ("so we can continue the momentum on this project").

2. *Ask how the other person works*. If your colleague wants to achieve inbox zero every day, email is probably not the best way to communicate. Figure out how your colleagues and managers enjoy working and try your best not to interrupt their productivity flow. Your colleague may prefer you to ping her on Skype or stop by her office versus sending an email, for instance. Bending to other people's processes will position you as a team player, not to mention make it easier for you to push your own projects through.

3. *Choose your battles*. There is a cost every time you engage in a workplace conflict and this cost is time. Projects get delayed and workers become stressed. Decide what your priorities are and let everything else go—even if you know you're right. The key is to know when you should push an idea and when you shouldn't. High performers know success is less about proving themselves, and more about contributing to a shared vision. Relationships reign supreme.

4. *Know that you're on the same team*. While the workplace can and should have multiple personalities and opinions, it's easy to forget that everyone is working toward the same objective. A colleague may not complete a task in the same way you would, but that's no reason to be divisive. You're all on the same team, working toward the same goal, and strong opinions are the sign of a passionate team; be grateful you're surrounded by people who care about their work as much as you do.

5. *Respect other people's expertise*. Most people just want to be heard and validated. Respect and acknowledge that your colleagues have an expertise that you don't. If you can understand not only that you don't know it all, but you can't do it all, you'll find it's much more enjoyable to interact with your co-workers and get things done. Try not to undermine people's authority and instead, ask for their input, feedback, and advice when something comes up in their realm of expertise. They'll appreciate being consulted, and you'll learn something new.

Working with different personalities isn't easy, but it's always necessary. Remember, you can't change how others behave, but you can use these five strategies to increase your own odds at success.

WORK ATTITUDES

How we behave at work often depends on how we feel about being there. Therefore, making sense of how people behave depends on understanding their work attitudes. An attitude refers to our opinions, beliefs, and feelings about aspects of our environment. We have attitudes toward the food we eat, people we meet, courses we take, and things we do. At work, two job attitudes have the greatest potential to influence how we behave. These are job satisfaction and organizational commitment.

Job satisfaction refers to the feelings people have toward their job. If the number of studies conducted on job satisfaction is an indicator, job satisfaction is probably the most important job attitude. Organizational commitment is the emotional attachment people have toward the company they work for. A highly committed employee is one who accepts and believes in the company's values, is willing to put out effort to meet the company's goals, and has a strong desire to remain with the company. People who are committed to their company often refer to their company as "we" as opposed to "they" as in "in this company, we have great benefits." The way we refer to the company indicates the type of attachment and identification we have with the company.

There is a high degree of overlap between job satisfaction and organizational commitment because things that make us happy with our job often make us more committed to the company as well. Companies believe that these attitudes are worth tracking because they often are associated with outcomes that are important to the Controlling role, such as performance, helping others, absenteeism, and turnover.

What Causes Positive Work Attitudes?

People pay attention to several factors of their work environment, including characteristics of the job (a function of Organizing activities), how they are treated (related to Leadership actions), the relationships they form with colleagues and managers (also Leadership related), and the level of stress the job entails.

Personality and values play important roles in how employees feel about their jobs. Factors

Contributing to Job Satisfaction and Organizational Commitment include:

- Personality
- Person-environment fit
- Job characteristics
- Psychological contract
- Organizational justice
- Work relationship
- stress

Job Characteristics

Employees tend to be more satisfied and committed in jobs that involve certain characteristics. The ability to use a variety of skills, having autonomy at work, receiving feedback on the job, and performing a significant task are some job characteristics that are related to satisfaction and commitment. However, the presence of these factors is not important for everyone. Some people have a high need for growth. These employees tend to be more satisfied when their jobs help them build new skills and improve.

Organizational Justice and the Psychological Contract

A strong influence over our satisfaction level is how fairly we are treated. People pay attention to the fairness of company policies and procedures, fair and kind treatment from supervisors, and fairness of their pay and other rewards they receive from the company. Organizational justice can be classified into three categories:

(1) procedural (fairness in the way policies and processes are carried out),
(2) distributive (the allocation of resources or compensation and benefits), and
(3) Interactional (the degree to which people are treated with dignity and respect). At the root of organizational justice is trust, something that is easier to break than to repair if broken.

The psychological contract is the unspoken, informal understanding that an employee will contribute certain things to the organization (e.g., work ability and a willing attitude) and will receive certain things in return (e.g., reasonable pay and benefits). Under the psychological contract, an employee may believe that if he or she works hard and receives favorable performance evaluations, he or she will receive an annual bonus, periodic raises and promotions, and will not be laid off. Since the "downsizing" trend of the past 20 years, many commentators have declared that the psychological contract is violated more often than not.

Relationships at Work

Two strong predictors of our happiness at work and commitment to the company are our relationships with coworkers and managers. The people we interact with, how friendly they are, whether we are socially accepted in our work group, whether we are treated with respect by them are important to our happiness at work. Research also shows that our relationship with our manager, how considerate the manager is, and whether we build a trust-based relationship with our manager are critically important to our job satisfaction and organizational commitment. When our manager and overall management listen to us, care about us, and value our opinions, we tend to feel good at work. When establishing effective relations with employees, little signals that you care about your employees go a long way. For example, in 2004 San Francisco's Hotel Carlton was taken over and renovated by a new management group, Joie de Vivre Hospitality. One of the small things the new management did that created dramatic results was that, in response to an employee attitude survey, they replaced the old vacuum cleaners housekeepers were using and started replacing them every year. It did not cost the company much to replace old machinery, but this simple act of listening to employee problems and taking action went a long way to make employees feel better.

Stress

Not surprisingly, the amount of stress present in a job is related to employee satisfaction and commitment. Stressors range from environmental ones (noise, heat, inadequate ventilation) to interpersonal ones (organizational politics, conflicts with coworkers) to organizational ones (pressure to avoid making mistakes, worrying about the security of the job). Some jobs, such as intensive care unit nurse and military fighter pilot, are inherently very stressful.

Another source of stress has to do with the roles people are expected to fulfill on and off the job. Role ambiguity is uncertainty about what our responsibilities are in the job. Role conflict involves contradictory demands at work; it can also involve conflict between fulfilling one's role as an employee and other roles in life, such as the role of parent, friend, or community volunteer.

Generally speaking, the higher the stress level, the lower job satisfaction tends to be. But not all stress is bad, and some stressors actually make us happier! For example, working under time pressure and having a high degree of responsibility are stressful, but they are also perceived as challenges and tend to be related to high levels of satisfaction.

CHAPTER TWO: APPLIED BEHAVIOR ANALYSIS

What is ABA?

The strategic and intentional application of scientific principles of human behavior and learning. The purpose is to:

- Predict, influence and modify the occurrence of certain behaviors.
- Teach or increase desired behaviors
- Reduce or eliminate undesired behaviors
- Analyze the environmental factors that influence behaviors, learning and motivation.

In behavior analysis, ABC data is typically the preferred method used when observing a behavior. This involves directly observing and recording situational factors surrounding a problem behavior using an assessment tool called ABC data collection. An ABC data form is an assessment tool used to gather information on a certain problem behavior or behaviors being exhibited by a child. ABC refers to:

> Antecedent- The events, action(s), or circumstances that occur immediately before a behavior

> Behavior- The behavior in detail

> Consequences- The action(s) or response(s) that immediately follows the behavior

What is an antecedent?

In technical terms, antecedents of behavior are stimulus events, situations, or circumstances that precede an operant response (Miltenberger, 2004). In Laymen terms, an antecedent is what was happening or what/who was present right before the behavior occurred.

Why are antecedents important?

- To understand and modify behavior, it's important to analyze the antecedents and consequences. When we understand the antecedents of a behavior we have information on the circumstances in which the behavior was reinforced and was punished (Miltenberger, 2004).
- Since behaviors tend to occur more in situations in which it has been reinforced and less in situations where it has been punished, having this valuable information helps us to predict

the situations and environments the behavior will be more likely to occur.

List of questions to ask to gather information on the antecedents of a problem behavior:
- When does the problem behavior usually occur?
- Where does the problem behavior usually occur?
- Who is present when the problem behavior occurs?
- What activities or events precede the occurrence of the problem behavior?
- What do other people say or do immediately before the problem behavior?
- Does the child engage in any other behaviors before the problem behavior?
- When, where, with whom, and in what circumstances is the problem behavior least likely to occur?

Improve Employee Performance With Behavior Modification

An important part of every manager's job is to guide employees toward activities that will help them make progress in their jobs, and away from activities that will derail them and negatively affect the organization. Through feedback and an effective rewards program (which may include, in some instances, punishment), managers can assist employees in getting to the best outcomes for their own careers and contributing to the performance of the organization.

What is behavior modification

Behavior modification is a method for encouraging employees to behave in ways that are considered desirable, and discouraging them from behaving in ways considered undesirable. It involves the variation of consequences resulting from a target behavior (contingent consequences). Consequences that strengthen a behavior are called reinforcement; consequences that weaken a behavior are called punishment.

Positive reinforcement involves giving employees something they value, for example, praising them for a job well done. By contrast, negative reinforcement involves taking away something that employees do not like, such as taking away probationary employment status.
Punishment also takes two forms: creating a negative consequence for employees (for example, a manager reprimanding an employee for arriving late to an important meeting); or taking

something positive away (for example, a manager taking away the employee's company car in the face of evidence that the employee used the company car, provided exclusively for business travel, for personal use).

Why it works

Behavior modification is based on the principles of operant conditioning developed by B.F. Skinner, who showed that behavior is a function of its consequences. People tend to repeat behaviors with favorable consequences and tend not to repeat behaviors with unfavorable consequences.

When a manager praises an employee for an excellent presentation, for example, the employee experiences this as a reward and will put time and attention into future presentations. However, if the manager appears to be displeased with the presentation and points out the information that was left out, the employee experiences this as a punishment and will try to put more effort and information into future presentations.

In some cases, however, the manager may have been happy with the presentation but was preoccupied and showed no response in the meeting, rushing out afterward without giving any feedback to the employee. This may be experienced as an unrewarding outcome and cause the employee to become discouraged. This could likely result in the employee putting less effort into future presentations.

N/B

Employees respond best to positive reinforcement (rewards). Rewards strengthen a behavior when employees see a strong connection between a specific behavior and a certain reward. To get the best results, managers need to clearly identify good performance in behavioral terms and reward those employees who engage in these specific behaviors.

To improve performance:

- Conduct training sessions to inform employees of the antecedents, behaviors, and consequences (see checklist) of the program. Identify a time frame and feedback methods.

- Give employees regular and helpful feedback as they embark on the process of behavior change.
- At the time specified, measure the target behaviors again and implement the program of rewards.

If outstanding customer service is the goal, a manager needs to tell employees what this looks like. Is it zero customer complaints in that quarter? Is it positive customer satisfaction surveys? What rating is considered positive on a five-point scale? Some managers may be happy with 4 out of 5 on the five-point scale, while others may only reward employees who receive 5 out of 5. Another consideration is how to respond to employees who receive customer complaints each quarter or who fail to meet standards on a continuous basis. For such employees, the manager needs to move to punishment, starting with reprimands, and then moving to a write-up, and so forth.

Again, for punishment to be effective, employees need to see a strong connection between the behavior and the punishment. Moreover, the manager needs to work with these underperforming employees to help them see what they are doing wrong and what they should be doing instead. The poor behavior needs to be specifically identified and the employee needs to be redirected to another, more desirable behavior.

Conclusion

Behavior modification has been shown to improve job performance, promote safe behaviors, reduce accidents, improve customer service, and assist employees in identifying and improving on a range of more functional behaviors in the workplace. For example, sales representatives have successfully implemented more effective sales techniques, manufacturing employees have raised their productivity levels, and customer service representatives have improved the level of support provided to customers.

CHAPTER THREE: EMPLOYEE MOTIVATION

What is motivation

Motivation is internal and external factors that stimulate desire and energy in people to be continually interested and committed to a job, role or subject, or to make an effort to attain a goal. Motivation can also be defined as the process that initiates, guides, and maintains goal-oriented behaviors. Motivation is what causes us to act, whether it is getting a glass of water to reduce thirst or reading a book to gain knowledge.

Motivation results from the interaction of both conscious and unconscious factors such as the (1) intensity of desire or need, (2) incentive or reward value of the goal, and (3) expectations of the individual and of his or her peers. These factors are the reasons one has for behaving a certain way. An example is a student that spends extra time studying for a test because he or she wants a better grade in the class.

Components of Motivation

Anyone who has ever had a goal (like wanting to lose ten pounds or wanting to run a marathon) probably immediately realizes that simply having the desire to accomplish something is not enough. Achieving such a goal requires the ability to persist through obstacles and endurance to keep going in spite of difficulties.

There are three major components to motivation: activation, persistence, and intensity.

1. *Activation* involves the decision to initiate a behavior, such as enrolling in a psychology class.

1. *Persistence* is the continued effort toward a goal even though obstacles may exist. An example of persistence would be taking more psychology courses in order to earn a degree although it requires a significant investment of time, energy, and resources.
2. *Intensity* can be seen in the concentration and vigor that goes into pursuing a goal. For example, one student might coast by without much effort, while another student will

study regularly, participate in discussions and take advantage of research opportunities outside of class. The first student lacks intensity, while the second pursues his educational goals with greater intensity.

Theories of motivation

Psychological Theories of Motivation to Increase Productivity

We all want to be more productive but getting motivated enough to actually get things done can seem impossible. Social scientists have been studying motivation for decades, trying to find out what motivates our behaviour, how and why.

Dozens of theories of motivation have been proposed over the years. Here are 5 popular theories of motivation that can help you increase workplace productivity...

1. Hertzberg's Two-Factor Theory

The Two-Factor Theory of motivation (otherwise known as dual-factor theory or motivation-hygiene theory) was developed by psychologist Frederick Herzberg in the 1950s.

Analyzing the responses of 200 accountants and engineers who were asked about their positive and negative feelings about their work, Herzberg found 2 factors that influence employee motivation and satisfaction...

1. **Motivator factors** – Simply put, these are factors that lead to satisfaction and motivate employees to work harder. Examples might include enjoying your work, feeling recognised and career progression.
2. **Hygiene factors** – These factors can lead to dissatisfaction and a lack of motivation if they are absent. Examples include salary, company policies, benefits, relationships with managers and co-workers.

According to Herzberg's findings, while motivator and hygiene factors both influenced motivation, they appeared to work completely independently of each other...

While motivator factors increased employee satisfaction and motivation, the absence of these factors didn't necessarily cause dissatisfaction. Likewise, the presence of hygiene factors didn't appear to increase satisfaction and motivation but their absence caused an increase in dissatisfaction.

How to apply it to the workplace

This theory implies that for the happiest and most productive workforce, you need to work on improving both motivator and hygiene factors.

To help motivate your employees, make sure they feel appreciated and supported. Give plenty of feedback and make sure your employees understand how they can grow and progress through the company.

To prevent job dissatisfaction, make sure that your employees feel that they are treated right by offering them the best possible working conditions and fair pay. Make sure you pay attention to your team and form supportive relationships with them.

Don't forget that all of your employees are different and what motivates one person might not motivate another. Paul Hebert of Symbolist believes that benefits packages should not be one-size-fits all…

"For true engagement to occur in a company you must first remove the issues that cause dissatisfaction – the baseline benefits offered by the company that satisfy the hygiene needs of the employee. Then you must focus on the individual and what they want out of their association with your enterprise."

2. Maslow's Hierarchy of Needs

The Hierarchy of Needs theory was coined by psychologist Abraham Maslow in his 1943 paper "A Theory of Human Motivation".

The crux of the theory is that individuals' most basic needs must be met before they become motivated to achieve higher level needs.

The hierarchy is made up of 5 levels:

1. **Physiological** – these needs must be met in order for a person to survive, such as food, water and shelter.
2. **Safety** – including personal and financial security and health and wellbeing.
3. **Love/belonging** – the need for friendships, relationships and family.
4. **Esteem** – the need to feel confident and be respected by others.
5. **Self-actualization** – the desire to achieve everything you possibly can and become the most that you can be.

According to the hierarchy of needs, you must be in good health, safe and secure with meaningful relationships and confidence before you are able to be the most that you can be.

How to apply it to the workplace

In order to get the most out of your team, you should also make sure you support them in other aspects of their lives outside work. Perhaps you could offer flexible working hours to give employees time to focus on their families and make sure they are paid fairly to help them feel financially stable.

3. Hawthorne Effect

The Hawthorne Effect was first described by Henry A. Landsberger in 1950 who noticed a tendency for some people to work harder and perform better when they were being observed by researchers.

The Hawthorne Effect is named after a series of social experiments on the influence of physical conditions on productivity at Western Electric's factory at Hawthorne, Chicago in the 1920s and 30s.

The researchers changed a number of physical conditions over the course of the experiments including lighting, working hours and breaks. In all cases, employee productivity increased when a change was made. The researchers concluded that employees became motivated to work harder as a response to the attention being paid to them, rather than the actual physical changes themselves.

How to apply it to the workplace

The Hawthorne Effect studies suggest that employees will work harder if they know they're being observed. While I don't recommend hovering over your employees watching them all day, you could try providing regular feedback, letting your team know that you know what they're up to and how they're doing.

Showing your employees that you care about them and their working conditions may also motivate them to work harder. Encourage your team to give you feedback and suggestions about their workspace and development.

4. Expectancy Theory

Expectancy Theory proposes that people will choose how to behave depending on the outcomes they expect as a result of their behaviour. In other words, we decide what to do based on what we expect the outcome to be. At work, it might be that we work longer hours because we expect a pay rise.

However, Expectancy Theory also suggests that the process by which we decide our behaviours is also influenced by how likely we perceive those rewards to be. In this instance, workers may be more likely to work harder if they had been promised a pay rise (and thus perceived that outcome as very likely) than if they had only assumed they might get one (and perceived the outcome as possible but not likely)

Expectancy Theory is based on three elements:

1. **Expectancy** – the belief that your effort will result in your desired goal. This is based on your past experience, your self-confidence and how difficult you think the goal is to achieve.
2. **Instrumentality** – the belief that you will receive a reward if you meet performance

expectations.

3. **Valence** – the value you place on the reward.

Therefore, according to Expectancy Theory, people are most motivated if they believe that they will receive a desired reward if they hit an achievable target. They are least motivated if they don't want the reward or they don't believe that their efforts will result in the reward.

How to apply it to the workplace

The key here is to set achievable goals for your employees and provide rewards that they actually want.

Rewards don't have to come in the form of pay rises, bonuses or all-expenses paid nights out (although I find these are usually welcomed!) Praise, opportunities for progression and "employee of the month" style rewards can all go a long way in motivating your employees.

Need some inspiration? Check out these 51 inexpensive ways to reward employees from author of The Toilet Paper Entrepreneur, Mike Michalowicz.

5. Three-Dimensional Theory of Attribution

Attribution Theory explains how we attach meaning to our own, and other people's behaviour. There are a number of theories about attribution.

Bernard Weiner's Three-Dimensional theory of attribution assumes that people try to determine why we do what we do. According to Weiner, the reasons we attribute to our behaviour can influence how we behave in the future.

For example, a student who fails an exam could attribute their failure to a number of factors and it's this attribution that will affect their motivation in the future.

Weiner theorized that specific attributions (e.g. bad luck, not studying hard enough) were less important than the characteristics of that attribution. According to Weiner, there are three main characteristics of attributions that can affect future motivation.

1. **Stability** – how stable is the attribution? For example, if the student believes they failed the exam because they weren't smart enough, this is a stable factor. An unstable factor is less permanent, such as being ill.

According to Weiner, stable attributions for successful achievements, such as passing exams, can lead to positive expectations, and thus higher motivation, for success in the future.

However, in negative situations, such as failing the exam, stable attributions can lead to lower expectations in the future.

2. **Locus of control** – was the event caused by an internal or an external factor?

For example, if the student believes it's their own fault they failed the exam, because they are innately not smart enough (an internal cause), they may be less motivated in the future. If they believed an external factor was to blame, such as poor teaching, they may not experience such a drop in motivation.

3. **Controllability** – how controllable was the situation? If an individual believes they could have performed better, they may be less motivated to try again in the future than someone who believes they failed because of factors outside of their control.

How to apply it to the workplace

Weiner's Three-Dimensional theory of attribution has implications for employee feedback.

Make sure you give your employees specific feedback, letting them know that you know they can improve and how they can about it. This, in theory, will help prevent them from attributing their failure to an innate lack of skill and see that success is controllable if they work harder or use different strategies.

You could also praise your employees for showing an improvement, even if the outcome was still not correct. For example, you might praise someone for using the correct methodology even though the results weren't what you wanted. This way, you are encouraging employees to attribute the failure to controllable factors, which again, can be improved upon in the future.

Significance/Importance of Motivation

Motivation is an integral part of the process of direction. While directing his subordinate, a manager must create and sustain in them the desire to work for the specified objectives:

1. High Efficiency:

A good motivational system releases the immense untapped reservoirs of physical and mental capabilities. A number of studies have shown that motivation plays a crucial role in determining the level of performance. "Poorly motivated people can nullify the soundest organisation." said Allen.

By satisfying human needs motivation helps in increasing productivity. Better utilisation of resources lowers cost of operations. Motivation is always goal directed. Therefore, higher the level of motivation, greater is the degree of goal accomplishment.

2. Better Image:

A firm that provides opportunities for financial and personal advancement has a better image in the employment market. People prefer to work for an enterprise because of opportunity for development, and sympathetic outlook. This helps in attracting qualified personnel and simplifies the staffing function.

3. Facilitates Change:

Effective motivation helps to overcome resistance to change and negative attitude on the part of employees like restriction of output. Satisfied workers take interest in new organisational goals and are more receptive to changes that management wants to introduce in order to improve efficiency of operations.

4. Human Relations:

Effective motivation creates job satisfaction which results in cordial relations between employer and employees. Industrial disputes, labour absenteeism and turnover are reduced with consequent benefits. Motivation helps to solve the central problem of management, i.e., effective use of human resources. Without motivation the workers may not put their best efforts and may seek satisfaction of their needs outside the organisation.

The success of any organisation depends upon the optimum utilisation of resources. The utilisation of physical resources depends upon the ability to work and the willingness to work of the employees. In practice, ability is not the problem but necessary will to work is lacking. Motivation is the main tool for building such a will. It is for this reason that Rensis Likert said, "Motivation is the core of management." It is the key to management in action.

Approaches to motivation

Five different approaches to explain motivation are:

- **The instinct approach**

Animals, including humans are born with a set of behaviour that steer us to act a certain way so that we could produce certain ends. These are called instincts. Some of these instincts are essential to our survival. This approach suggests that we are born to be motivated. However, there are many questions that this approach cannot answer, e.g. what and how many instincts exist.

- **The drive-reduction approach**

This approach suggests that our body has a tendency to act in such a way that a steady internal state is maintained. This tendency is called homeostasis. For example, if you are hungry, you are motivated to look for food to reduce your hunger drive.

There are 2 types of drives:

1) Primary drives – these are related to our biological needs, e.g. hunger, thirst, etc.

2) Secondary drives – these are related to our prior experience and learning, e.g. achievement.

- **The arousal approach**

This approach came about because there were situations which the drive-reduction approach could not explain. In some way, this approach is similar to the drive-reduction approach. The arousal approach to motivation suggests that if our excitement level is too high, we try to reduce it. If our excitement level is too low, we try to increase it by seeking stimulation.

- **The incentive approach**

Simply put, we are motivated to get what we want. For example, students want good grades so they study hard.

- **The cognitive approach**

The cognitive approach to motivation suggests that we are motivated by our thoughts, expectations and goals.

There are 2 types of motivations:

1) Intrinsic motivation; We do things because we enjoy doing them. For example, we exercise because it feels good to exercise.

2) Extrinsic motivation; We do things because of the tangible rewards, e.g. good grades, money, etc. For example, we exercise because we want to lose weight.

We should be highly motivated if we get paid to do what we love, right? This is not necessarily true because extrinsic motivation can sometimes undermine intrinsic motivation. In one study, children who really enjoyed drawing were either promised or not promised a reward for their drawing. It was found that children who were promised a reward were less likely to draw again later.

Maslow's hierarchy of needs

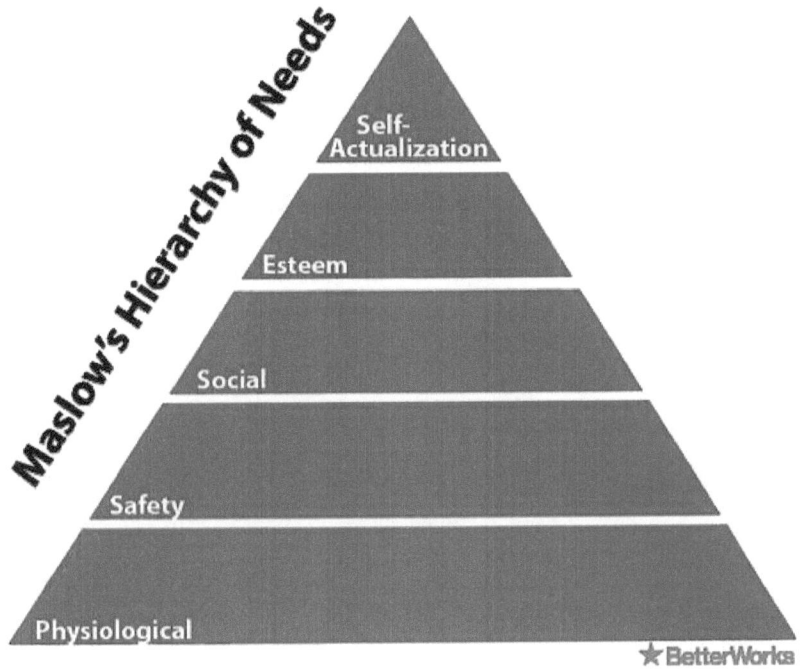

Abraham Maslow, a psychologist, came up with a model of motivation. The model suggests that we are motivated to satisfy our needs in a "bottom-up" manner. We first satisfy our physiological needs such as water and food. When these needs are satisfied, we move up to the second level, which is our need to be safe, and so on. Only after the needs at the lower 4 levels are met can we strive for self-actualization, which is a state of self-fulfillment.

5 Easy Ways To Motivate - And Demotivate - Employees

I'll put it as simply as I can: There are an awful lot of unmotivated employees out there. With a recent national study showing that less than 1 in 4 non-management employees is fully engaged (aka, fully motivated and productive), there is, shall we say, ample room for improvement. And since an employee's relationship with his or her direct manager is *the* single most important factor influencing engagement, the responsibility falls to management to improve motivational levels. Accordingly, here are 5 easy ways to motivate – and demotivate – employees.

1. Align individual economic interests with company performance – Okay, so this first one isn't quite as easy as the others; it does take more doing at the highest management levels than the rest. But incentive compensation programs that give employees *at all levels* of an organization a chance to benefit when a company prospers… can naturally boost motivation (always assuming solid individual performance in order for one to share in financial rewards)

2. Take a genuine interest in the future path of an employee's career – It does wonders for an employee's attitude to believe that a manager really cares about where his or her career is headed. Mentoring, coaching, suggesting additional training or coursework - all of these can be helpful to employees, and highly valued.

3. Take a genuine interest in their work-life balance – To the extent that managers can offer some flexibility in schedules… and be understanding about family commitments, doctors' appointments and so on – such sensitivity can be greatly appreciated. Small gestures often make a big difference.

4. Listen - This is an easy one: Just listen thoughtfully. To employees' ideas for job improvement… or their problems, concerns, frustrations, conflicts, dramas, kids' issues, parents' issues, grandparents' issues – you name it, I've heard it. Okay, so you do have to separate the wheat from the chaff and as a manager it can wear you out at times – but within reason, intelligent listening is an integral part of the job. (If someone is a chronic malingerer, and carps for the sake of carping, just tell them to knock it off and get back to work. But if someone is a good employee… well, people appreciate being heard.)

5. Do unto others as you would have done unto you - When it comes to treatment of subordinates, this is as basic as it gets. But powerful too – still as valid today as it was a few thousand years ago. It shows you respect your employees as individuals, and for the job they do.

Now about those easy ways to **demotivate** *someone…*

1. Use your positional power as a manager in a way that shows you don't fully respect your employees as individuals - This is the reverse of number 5 and it can be subtle. Be chronically late for employee meetings. Don't return their messages. Ignore their suggestions for how to improve operations. These may seem like small things to an executive with weightier issues on his or her mind... but the reality is people resent them. As noted above, small things can make a big difference in one's feelings about work.

2. Take credit for a project one of your employees actually did most of the work on - This is guaranteed to make people crazy. Good managers are secure enough to give full credit where it's due.

3. Lose your temper - A nasty cousin of number 1) above. It's just human nature: People dislike being on the wrong end of this sort of thing. Lost tempers are often followed by lost loyalty.

4. Don't stand up for your employees when under personal or organizational attack - Assuming the attacks aren't merited – just personal or organizational nonsense (which *has* been known to occur) – your employees will want and expect you to back them up. If you don't, they'll remember it.

5. Be emotionally stingy - People like praise. They *want* to know they're doing a good job and are valued. (Assuming they *are* doing a good job, of course. If they're not, then telling them they are does nothing except erode your credibility.) But if they are doing well, simple words of encouragement are easy, inexpensive and can be motivational.

All of these suggestions (other than the first one on aligning economic interests) have the same cost: nothing. And this list is by no means all-inclusive. When it comes to motivating employees, you're limited only by your imagination.

CHAPTER FOUR: WORK STRESS AND PSYCHOLOGICAL WELL-BEING

What is psychological well-being?

Psychological well-being refers to how people evaluate their lives. According to Diener (1997), these evaluations may be in the form of cognitions or in the form of affect. The cognitive part is an information based appraisal of one's life that is when a person gives conscious evaluative judgments about one's satisfaction with life as a whole. The affective part is a hedonic evaluation guided by emotions and feelings such as frequency with which people experience pleasant/unpleasant moods in reaction to their lives. The assumption behind this is that most people evaluate their life as either good or bad, so they are normally able to offer judgments. Further, people invariably experience moods and emotions, which have a positive effect or a negative effect. Thus, people have a level of subjective well-being even if they do not often consciously think about it, and the psychological system offers virtually a constant evaluation of what is happening to the person

Six Domains of Psychological Well-being

As scholars of the topic know, happiness and well-being are complicated constructs. This was evident this past weekend as my family engaged in a spirited discussion on the question what makes people happy and what constitutes happiness. One thing that they got hung up on, which is an area that scholars have debated much about, is the difference and relationship between being happy and optimal psychological functioning. As such, I thought it would be useful to share what I call "Ryff's Six", which is a helpful model for thinking about optimal psychological functioning. I have framed her work below in the form of an assessment, so that readers can get a better sense of applying her "six" to themselves and seeing what areas they are doing better at than others.

Six Dimensions of Psychological Well-Being

Do you agree or disagree with each of the following statements:

1. Many of my personal qualities trouble me enough that I wish I could change them.
2. I feel isolated and frustrated in interpersonal relationships.

3. When making important decisions, I rely on the judgments of others.
4. Often I am unable to change or improve my circumstances.
5. My life lacks meaning.
6. I have a sense of personal stagnation that often leaves me bored.

These six statements represent psychological well-being:[1]

- Self-acceptance - positive evaluations of oneself;
- Positive interpersonal relations - close, warm relationships with others;
- Autonomy - self-determination;
- Environmental mastery - sense of effectiveness in mastering circumstances and challenges;
- Purpose in life - a sense of meaning that gives one's life a sense of direction and purpose;
- Personal growth - improvement and growth.

Your response on each of these dimensions reflects your self-functioning and psychological well-being. To be well psychologically is to possess positive self-regard, positive relationships, autonomy, mastery, purpose, and a trajectory of growth. Your answers to these questions reveal how well or how poorly you are doing in maintaining your well-being.

It is not enough to only do well in one of the areas of well-being. It is important to maintain balance in all of the areas of your well-being. Here are the Six Dimensions of Psychological Well-Being that you can use to see how well you are doing:

Self-Acceptance

High scorer: possesses a positive attitude toward the self; acknowledges and accepts multiple aspects of self, including good and bad qualities; feels positive about the past.   *Low scorer*: feels dissatisfied with self; is disappointed with what has occurred in past life; is troubled about certain qualities; wishes to be different than what he or she is.

Positive Relations with Others

High scorer: has warm, satisfying, trusting relationships with others; is concerned about the welfare of others; capable of strong empathy, affection, and intimacy; understands give-and-take of human relationships.   *Low scorer*: has few close, trusting relationships with others; finds it difficult to be warm, open, and concerned about others; is isolated and frustrated in interpersonal relationships; is not willing to make compromises; sustain important ties with others.

Autonomy

High scorer: is self-determining; is able to resist social pressures to think and act in certain ways; regulates behavior from within; evaluates self by personal standards.   *Low scorer*: is concerned about the expectations and evaluations of others; relies on judgments of others to make important decisions; conforms to social pressures to think and act in certain ways.

Environmental Mastery

High scorer: has a sense of mastery and competence in managing the environment; controls complex array of external activities; makes effective use of surrounding opportunities; is able to choose or create contexts suitable to personal needs and values.   *Low scorer*: has difficulty managing everyday affairs; feels unable to change or improve surrounding context; is unaware of surrounding opportunities; lacks sense of control over external world.

Purpose in Life

High scorer: Have goals in life and a sense of directedness; feels there is meaning to present and past life; holds beliefs that give life purpose; has aims and objectives for living.   *Low scorer*: lacks a sense of meaning in life; has few goals or aims; lacks a sense of direction; does not see purpose in the past; have no outlooks or beliefs that give life meaning.

Personal Growth

High scorer: has a feeling of continued development; sees self as growing and expanding; is open to new experiences; has sense of realizing his or her potential; sees improvement in self and behavior over time; is changing in ways that reflect more self-knowledge and effectiveness.   *Low scorer*: has a sense of personal stagnation; lacks sense of improvement or expansion over time; feels bored and uninterested with life; feels unable to develop new attitudes or behaviors.

Employee Stress

What is stress?

Stress is your body's way of responding to any kind of demand or threat. When you feel threatened, your nervous system responds by releasing a flood of stress hormones, including adrenaline and cortisol, which rouse the body for emergency action. Your heart pounds faster, muscles tighten, blood pressure rises, breath quickens, and your senses become sharper. These physical changes increase your strength and stamina, speed your reaction time, and enhance your focus. This is known as "fight or flight" or the mobilization stress response and is your body's way of protecting you. There is also a "freeze" or immobilization response that occurs if we become traumatized.

Stress within your comfort zone can help you perform under pressure, motivate you to do your best, even keep you safe when danger looms. But when stress becomes overwhelming, it can damage your mood and relationships, and lead to a host of serious mental and physical health problems. The trouble is that modern life is so full of frustrations, deadlines, and demands that many of us don't even realize how stressed we are. By recognizing the symptoms and causes of stress, you can take the first steps to reducing its harmful effects and improving your quality of life.

When stress is within your comfort zone, it can help you to stay focused, energetic, and alert. In emergency situations, stress can save your life—giving you extra strength to defend yourself, for example, or spurring you to slam on the brakes to avoid an accident. Stress can also help you rise to meet challenges. Stress is what keeps you on your toes during a presentation at work, sharpens your concentration when you're attempting the game-winning free throw, or drives you to study for an exam when you'd rather be watching TV. But beyond your comfort zone, stress stops being helpful and can start causing major damage to your mind and body.

The effects of chronic stress

The body's nervous system often does a poor job of distinguishing between daily stressors and life-threatening events. If you're stressed over an argument with a friend, a traffic jam on your commute, or a mountain of bills, for example, your body can still react as if you're facing a life-or-death situation.

When you repeatedly experience the mobilization or fight-or-flight stress response in your daily life, it can lead to serious health problems. Chronic stress disrupts nearly every system in your body. It can shut down your immune system, upset your digestive and reproductive systems, raise blood pressure, increase the risk of heart attack and stroke, speed up the aging process and leave you vulnerable to many mental and physical health problems.

Health problems caused or exacerbated by stress include:

1. Depression and anxiety
2. Weight problems
3. Auto immune diseases
4. Skin conditions, such as eczema
5. Reproductive issues
6. Pain of any kind
7. Heart disease
8. Digestive problems
9. Sleep problems
10. Cognitive and memory problems

Signs and symptoms of chronic stress or stress overload

The following table lists some of the common warning signs and symptoms of chronic stress. The more signs and symptoms you notice in yourself, the closer you may be to stress overload.

Cognitive Symptoms
- Memory problems
- Inability to concentrate
- Poor judgment

- Seeing only the negative
- Anxious or racing thoughts
- Constant worrying

Emotional Symptoms
- Depression or general unhappiness
- Anxiety and agitation
- Moodiness, irritability, or anger
- Feeling overwhelmed
- Loneliness and isolation
- Other mental or emotional health problems

Physical Symptoms
- Aches and pains
- Diarrhea or constipation
- Nausea, dizziness
- Chest pain, rapid heartbeat
- Loss of sex drive
- Frequent colds or flu

Behavioral Symptoms
- Eating more or less
- Sleeping too much or too little
- Withdrawing from others
- Procrastinating or neglecting responsibilities
- Using alcohol, cigarettes, or drugs to relax
- Nervous habits (e.g. nail biting, pacing)

Causes of stress

The situations and pressures that cause stress are known as stressors. We usually think of stressors as being negative, such as an exhausting work schedule or a rocky relationship.

However, anything that puts high demands on you can be stressful. This includes positive events such as getting married, buying a house, going to college, or receiving a promotion.

Of course, not all stress is caused by external factors. Stress can also be internal or self-generated, when you worry excessively about something that may or may not happen, or have irrational, pessimistic thoughts about life.

Common external causes of stress

1. Major life changes
2. Work or school
3. Relationship difficulties
4. Financial problems
5. Being too busy
6. Children and family

Common internal causes of stress

1. Chronic worry
2. Pessimism
3. Rigid thinking, lack of flexibility
4. Negative self-talk
5. Unrealistic expectations/Perfectionism
6. All-or-nothing attitude

Types of organizational stress

These sources of stress come in different degrees and can be broadly categorized into four distinct types. Understanding the different types of stress is the first step to identifying the signs and symptoms both in oneself and in others. Dr. Albrecht, in his book titled "u0098Stress and the Manager', identifies the four types of stress that occur at the work place. These include:

a. **Time Stress:** This is where individuals lack enough time to complete all of their assigned duties. Such individuals agonize and are bothered by the number of things they are supposed to do (Albrecht, 2010). Hence, they worry and fear that they will, at some point, fail to do something important. In essence, such workers feel trapped, hopeless and unhappy about their status. Workers under this type of stress worry about deadlines and most of the time rush to avoid being late (Fried, 2008).

b. **Anticipatory Stress**: This describes the stress that workers experience regarding the future. The basic premise is that workers naturally worry about the fact that something might go wrong in the near future. Albrecht, (2010) asserts that such stress is usually focused on a particular event or occurrence within the organization which directly impact him/her but for which he/she has no control or influence over. This type of stress can sometimes be undefined and vague owing to how individuals foresee their own future. For example, being concerned about a service an individual is responsible for getting hacked. Or, it can be more specific and based on associations an individual makes regarding his particular status and one or more historical precedents within the organization.

c. **Situational Stress**: Situational stress occurs when individuals are in an intimidating situation over which they have no control. Most of the time, this occurs due to a crisis that happens in the organization. Such situations may involve a conflict of interest, loss of acceptance or change is status in an individual's group. For instance, consider a situation where admin staffs are asked by management to make changes to a system at the expense of security safeguards to enable some functionality. The staff whose recommendations have been disregarded will experience situational stress as they execute a task they know is detrimental to the welfare of the organization. Moreover, when individuals make major mistakes in front of the management and/or their colleagues, it makes them stressed (Albrecht, 2010).

d. **Encounter Stress:** This type of stress revolves around individual contacts. People get stressed when they are anxious about interacting with a particular group of individuals or a particular person (Albrecht, 2010). It often occurs in a situation where workers interact with clients or customers who may be in some form of distress. Physicians and social workers are very familiar with this kind of stress because of the kinds of people they deal with. Equally stressful is an interaction by an employee with the incident handling team following a compromise or security incident. Especially if the employee is worried s/he will be held, even if partly, responsible for the incident. On the flip side, contact overload can also lead to this form of stress. Consider your incident handler having to continually meet with employees on the defensive, distrusting the incident handling team's intent.

Stress tolerance: How much stress is too much?

We're all different. Some people seem to be able to roll with life's punches, while others tend to crumble in the face of small obstacles or frustrations. Some people even thrive on the excitement of a high-stress lifestyle. For example, your morning commute may make you anxious and tense because you worry that traffic will make you late. Others, however, may find the trip relaxing because they allow more time and enjoy listening to music while they drive.

Factors that influence your stress tolerance

Your resiliency to stress depends on many factors, but there are steps you can take to improve your tolerance and handle more setbacks and challenges without becoming overwhelmed by stress.

- **Emotional awareness.** Many of us are so used to being overloaded with stress that we don't even notice it anymore. Feeling stressed feels *normal*. But awareness of what you're feeling, physically and emotionally, can have a profound effect on both your stress tolerance and how you go about reducing stress. Having the emotional awareness to recognize when you're stressed and then being able to calm and soothe yourself can increase your tolerance to stress and help you bounce back from adversity.
- **The quality of your relationships and support network.** Social engagement has always been a human being's most evolved response to life's stressors. So it's no surprise that people with a strong network of friends and family—with whom they're comfortable sharing emotions—are better able to tolerate stress. On the flip side, the more lonely and isolated you are, the less opportunity you have for social engagement and the greater your vulnerability to stress.
- **Physical activity.** Regular exercise can lift your mood and serve as a distraction to your worries, allowing you to find some quiet time and break out of the cycle of negative thoughts that feed stress and anxiety.

- **Diet.** The food you eat can improve or worsen your mood and affect your ability to cope with life's stressors. Eating a diet full of processed and convenience food, refined carbohydrates, and sugary snacks can worsen symptoms of stress while eating a diet rich in fresh fruit and vegetables, high-quality protein, and **healthy fats**, especially omega-3 fatty acids, can help you better cope with life's ups and downs.

Other factors that influence your stress tolerance

- **Your sense of control** – It's easier to take stress in your stride if you have confidence in your ability to influence events and persevere through challenges. This is why hardship or persistent money worries can be major stressors for so many of us. If you feel like things are out of your control, you're likely to have less tolerance for stress.
- **Your attitude and outlook** – Hopeful people are often more stress-hardy. They tend to embrace challenges, have a stronger sense of humor, and accept change as an inevitable part of life.
- **Your knowledge and preparation** – The more you know about a stressful situation, including how long it will last and what to expect, the easier it is to cope. For example, if you go into surgery with a realistic picture of what to expect post-op, a painful recovery will be less stressful than if you were expecting to bounce back immediately.

Improving your ability to handle stress

Whether you're trying to build your tolerance to stress or cope with its symptoms, you have much more control over stress than you might think. Unfortunately, many of us try to deal with stress in ways that only compound the problem. We drink too much to unwind at the end of a stressful day, fill up on comfort food, zone out in front of the TV for hours, use pills to relax, or lash out at other people. However, there are many healthier and more effective ways to cope with stress and its symptoms.

1. **Get moving**

This is something you can do right now to help yourself start to feel better: exercise. Activities that require moving both your arms and your legs are particularly effective at managing stress.

Rhythmic exercises such as walking, running, swimming, dancing, and aerobic classes are good choices, especially if you exercise mindfully (focusing your attention on the physical sensations you experience as you move). If you've been traumatized or experienced the immobilization stress response, mindfully exercising in this way can help you to become "unstuck" and move on.

2. Connect to others

The simple act of talking face to face with another human can trigger hormones that relieve stress when you're feeling uncomfortable, unsure, or unsafe. Even just a brief exchange of kind words or a friendly look from another human being can help calm and soothe your nervous system. Being helpful and friendly to others delivers stress-reducing pleasure as well as providing great opportunities to expand your social network.

3. Engage your senses

Another fast way to relieve stress is by engaging one or more of your senses—sight, sound, taste, smell, touch, or movement. The key is to find the sensory input that works for you. Does listening to an uplifting song make you feel calm? Or smelling ground coffee? Or maybe petting an animal works quickly to make you feel centered? Everyone responds to sensory input a little differently, so experiment to find what works best for you. Read: Stress Relief in the Moment

4. Set aside relaxation time

Relaxation techniques such as yoga, meditation, and deep breathing activate the body's relaxation response, a state of restfulness that is the opposite of the fight or flight or mobilization stress response.

5. Eat a healthy diet

Eating a healthy diet isn't about eating bland food, adhering to strict dietary limitations, or depriving yourself of the foods you love. But by re-examining your existing diet and experimenting with new ways of eating that promote mental health, you can find an eating plan that not only helps to relieve stress, but also boosts your energy, improves your outlook, and stabilizes your mood.

6. Get your rest

Feeling tired can increase stress by causing you to think irrationally. At the same time, chronic stress can disrupt your sleep. Whether you're having trouble falling asleep or staying asleep at night, there are plenty of ways to improve your sleep so you feel less stressed and more productive and emotionally balanced

CHAPTER FIVE: CAREERS AND CAREER MANAGEMENT

Career management is lifelong, self-monitored process of career planning that involves choosing and setting personal goals, and formulating strategies for achieving them. Career Management ensures others know about you and your value. Career management is a continuous process that occurs throughout one's career and not just at discrete times. It may be helpful to think of career management as a philosophy and set of habits that will enable you to achieve career goals and develop career resiliency.

Successful career management is accomplished through regular habits of building relationships, engaging in career development conversations, updating your career development plan, and setting new goals as life and career needs change. Being proficient at career management also means possessing basic skills related to job searching and managing changes in a resilient manner.

What is Career Management Planning?
In the most basic of terms, a career management plan is very similar to a financial plan and focuses on your *assets* (skills, strengths, experience, qualifications), *your liabilities* (weaknesses, threats to industry), *goals* (life, career, financial, family) and *strategy* (timetables, strategic actions, tactics). It is a tool that becomes your guideline to working through this unsettled and often changing environment. Most important, it puts you in control of your career – and is proactive versus reactive.

Every professional should have some level of career management plan – especially those on the professional & executive level where this is an absolute must-have. The need for a plan is heightened by the exposure and risk you take in your career or job. For example, a fifth grade teacher who has taught for 30 years who has contributed greatly to the lives of students may not need this; an educator who has developed leading-edge programs and initiatives and is seeking that next level in their educational career would be a candidate. The business owner ready to cash out, sell their business and pursue other options is clearly a candidate; many skilled craftspeople likely would not have a need as their plan is largely dictated by the profession.

The Process of Career Management Planning

Defining the process of engaging and developing a career management plan can be summarized in three distinct elements: *Discover, Plan & Act.*

- *Discover* -Accomplished through 1-on-1 discussion, assessments, situation analysis and market studies, the initial focus is discovering skills, core competencies and future opportunities aligned with personal and professional goals.

- *Plan* -The process then moves to developing the plan inclusive of goals with specific timelines (Position – Role – Responsibility – Compensation – Culture) and planned actions to achieve the goals.

- *Act* – It is then time to act. Working again 1-on-1, short term goals and actions are planned with measurable accountability reviewed through coaching & mentoring executive sessions normally scheduled on a monthly, quarterly or semi-annual basis, depending upon needs.

Each need is unique and therefore, the process utilized is planned to align with goals and needs.

The Elements of a Career Management Plan

Like a financial plan, a career management plan is inclusive of:

- Inventory of Assets, Skills and Core Competencies

- Defined and measurable career goals & metrics: 1, 3, 5 & 10 years (for some)
- Identification of career direction & opportunities
- Current & Projected career market analysis
- Compensation plan
- Strategic career management plan: Strategy, actions, timetables
- Marketing strategy: Branding, networks, resources, tools (resumes, letters, strategic career statements).

Some elect to do this on their own. Others will work with an expert who will help craft the plan. Then it is measurement and accountability – being sure you are hitting your stated goals and actions.

With a clearly defined career management plan you will have the *clarity, courage and confidence* to take your career and life to a level you never expected. You will never have to worry about the "what if" – you will have a plan to address each and every change and turn that can be presented to you.

Short-Term Career Planning

A short-term career plan focuses on a timeframe ranging from the coming year to the next few years, depending on the job-seeker. The key characteristic of short-term career planning is developing realistic goals and objectives that you can accomplish in the near future.

As you begin your career planning, take the time to free yourself from all career barriers. What are career barriers? There are personal barriers (such as lack of motivation, apathy, laziness, or procrastination), family pressure (such as expectations to work in the family business, follow a certain career path, or avoidance of careers that are below your status/stature), and peer pressure. And while career planning and career decision-making is an important aspect of your life, do not put so much pressure on yourself that it paralyzes you from making any real choices, decisions, or plans. Finally, career planning is an ever-changing and evolving process — or journey — so take it slowly and easily.

To help you with your career planning, consider using the following exercises to their fullest potential.

Career Planning Exercises:

1. Analyze your current/future lifestyle. Are you happy with your current lifestyle? Do you want to maintain it or change it? Be sure to identify the key characteristics of your ideal lifestyle. Does your current career path allow you the lifestyle you seek?

2. Analyze your likes/dislikes. What kinds of activities — both at work and at play — do you enjoy? What kind of activities do you avoid? Make a list of both types of activities. Now take a close look at your current job and career path in terms of your list of likes and dislikes. Does your current job have more likes or dislikes?

3. Analyze your passions. Reflect on the times and situations in which you feel most passionate, most energetic, most engaged – and see if you can develop a common profile of these situations. Develop a list of your passions. How many of these times occur while you are at work?

4. Analyze your strengths and weaknesses. Step back and look at yourself from an employer's perspective. What are your strengths? What are your weaknesses? Think in terms of work experience, education/training, skill development, talents and abilities, technical knowledge, and personal characteristics.

5. Analyze your definition of success. Spend some time thinking about how you define success. What is success to you: wealth, power, control, contentment...

6. Analyze your personality. Are you an extravert or an introvert? Do you like thinking or doing? Do you like routines or change? Do you like sitting behind the desk or being on the move? Take the time to analyze yourself first, then take one or more of these self-assessment tests.

7. Analyze your dream job. Remember those papers you had to write as a kid about what you wanted to be when you grew up? Take the time to revert back to those idyllic times and brainstorm about your current dream job; be sure not to let any negative thoughts cloud your thinking. Look for ideas internally, but also make the effort to explore/research other careers/occupations that interest you.

8. Analyze your current situation. Before you can even do any planning, clearly and realistically identify your starting point.

Once you've completed these exercises, the next step is to develop a picture of yourself and your career over the next few years. Once you've developed the mental picture, the final step is developing a plan for achieving your goal.

Career Planning Steps:

1. Identify your next career move. If you have been examining multiple career paths, now is the time to narrow down the choices and focus on one or two careers.
2. Conduct detailed career research and gather information on the careers that most interest you.
3. Pinpoint the qualifications you need to move to the next step in your career or to make the move to a new career path. If you're not sure, search job postings and job ads, conduct informational interviews, research job descriptions.
4. Compare your current profile with the qualifications developed in step 3. How far apart are the two profiles? If fairly well-matched, it may be time to switch to a job-search. If fairly far apart, can you realistically achieve the qualifications in the short-term? If yes, move to the next step; if no, consider returning to the first step.
5. Develop a plan to get qualified. Make a list of the types of qualifications you need to enhance your standing for your next career move, such as receiving additional training, certification, or experience. Develop a timeline and action plans for achieving each type, being sure to set specific goals and priorities.

Long-Term Career Planning

Long-term career planning usually involves a planning window of five years or longer and involves a broader set of guidelines and preparation. Businesses, careers, and the workplace are rapidly changing, and the skills that you have or plan for today may not be in demand years from now. Long-range career planning should be more about identifying and developing core skills that employers will always value while developing your personal and career goals in broad strokes.

Core Workplace Skills: communications (verbal and written), critical and creative thinking, teamwork and team-building, listening, social, problem-solving, decision-making, interpersonal, project management, planning and organizing, computer/technology, and commitment to continuous/lifelong learning.

Identifying Career/Employment Trends: How can you prepare for future career changes and developments? The best way is to stay active in short-term career planning. By regularly scanning the environment and conducting research on careers, you'll quickly become an expert on the career paths that interest you — and you'll be better prepared for your next move.

CHAPTER SIX: JOB DESIGN AND NEW TECHNOLOGY

Job design (also referred to as **work design** or **task design**) is a core function of human resource management and it is related to the specification of contents, methods and relationship of jobs in order to satisfy technological and organizational requirements as well as the social and personal requirements of the job holder. Its principles are geared towards how the nature of a person's job affects their attitudes and behavior at work, particularly relating to characteristics such as skill variety and autonomy. The aim of a job design is to improve *job satisfaction*, to improve through-put, to improve quality and to reduce employee problems (e.g., grievances, absenteeism).

Job design techniques

1. Job rotation

Job rotation is a job design method which is able to enhance motivation, develop workers' outlook, increase productivity, improve the organization's performance on various levels by its multi-skilled workers, and provides new opportunities to improve the attitude, thought, capabilities and skills of workers. Job rotation is also a process by which employees laterally mobilize and serve their tasks in different organizational levels; when an individual experiences different posts and responsibilities in an organization, ability increases to evaluate his capabilities in the organization.

2. Job enlargement

Hulin and Blood (1968) define *Job enlargement* as the process of allowing individual workers to determine their own pace (within limits), to serve as their own inspectors by giving them responsibility for quality control, to repair their own mistakes, to be responsible for their own machine set-up and repair, and to attain choice of method. Frederick Herzberg referred to the addition of interrelated tasks as 'horizontal job loading'.

3. Job enrichment

Job enrichment increases the employees' autonomy over the planning and execution of their own work. Job enrichment has the same motivational advantages of job enlargement; however it has the added benefit of granting workers autonomy. Frederick Herzberg viewed job enrichment as 'vertical job loading' because it also includes tasks formerly performed by someone at a higher level where planning and control are involved.

4. Scientific management

Under *scientific management* people would be directed by reason and the problems of industrial unrest would be appropriately (i.e., scientifically) addressed. This philosophy is oriented toward the maximum gains possible to employees. Managers would guarantee that their subordinates would have access to the maximum of economic gains by means of rationalized processes. Organizations were portrayed as rationalized sites, designed and managed according to a rule of rationality imported from the world of technique.

5. Human Relations School

The *Human Relations School* takes the view that businesses are social systems in which psychological and emotional factors have a significant influence on productivity. The common elements in human relations theory are the beliefs that

- Performance can be improved by good human relations
- Managers should consult employees in matters that affect staff
- Leaders should be democratic rather than authoritarian
- Employees are motivated by social and psychological rewards and are not just "economic animals"
- The work group plays an important part in influencing performance

6. Socio-technical systems

Socio-technical systems aims on jointly optimizing the operation of the social and technical system; the good or service would then be efficiently produced and psychological needs of the workers fulfilled. Embedded in Socio-technical Systems are motivational assumptions, such as intrinsic and extrinsic rewards.

7. Work reform

Work reform states about the workplace relation and the changes made which are more suitable to management and employee to encourage increased workforce participation.

8. Motivational work design

The psychological literature on employee motivation contains considerable evidence that job design can influence satisfaction, motivation and job performance. It influences them primarily because it affects the relationship between the employee's expectancy that increased performance will lead to rewards and the preference of different rewards for the individual.

Hackman and Oldman developed the theory that a workplace can be redesigned to greater improve their core job characteristics. Their overall concept consists of:

- Making larger work units by combining smaller, more specialized tasks.
- Mandating worker(s) to be responsible via having direct contact with clients.
- Having employee evaluations done frequently in order to provide feedback for learning.
- Allowing workers to be responsible for their job by giving them authority and control.

CHAPTER SEVEN: UNDER-EMPLOYMENT AND SKILLS UTILIZATION

What is 'Underemployment?'

Underemployment is a measure of employment and labor utilization in the economy that looks at how well the labor force is being utilized in terms of skills, experience and availability to work. Labor that falls under the underemployment classification includes those workers who are highly skilled but working in low paying jobs, workers who are highly skilled but working in low skill jobs and part-time workers who would prefer to be full time. This is different from unemployment in that the individual is working but is not working at his full capability

Underemployment describes the employment of workers with high skill levels and postsecondary education who are working in relatively low-skilled, low-wage jobs. For example, someone with a college degree may be tending bar, or working as a factory assembly line worker. This may result from the existence of unemployment, which makes workers with bills to pay (and responsibilities) take almost any jobs available, even if they do not use their full talents. This can also occur with individuals who are being discriminated against, lack appropriate trade certification or academic degrees (such as a high school or college diploma), have disabilities or mental illnesses, or have served time in prison.

Two common situations which can lead to underemployment are immigrants and new graduates. When highly trained immigrants arrive in a country, their foreign credentials may not be recognized or accepted in their new country, or they may have to do a lengthy or costly re-credentialing process. As a result, when doctors or engineers from other countries immigrate, they may be unable to work in their profession, and they may have to seek menial work. New graduates may also face underemployment, because even though they have completed the technical training for a given field for which there is a good job market, they lack experience. So a recent graduate with a master's degree in accounting or business administration may have to work in a low-paid job as a barista or store clerk until able to find work in their field.

Karl Marx predicted that mass unemployment would become the salient characteristic of labor markets in advanced economies as machines were increasingly substituted for human workers. It is not clear that pattern is as inevitable as Marx forecast. But *under*employment (working at less than one's full productive capacities) seems to be the hallmark of the modern workforce. Over the last 50 years, there has been an inexorable trend of college graduates taking jobs that were previously filled by workers with lower educational credentials. Today, some 48 percent of college-educated men and women have jobs—such as bank tellers, waiters, taxi drivers, and coffee baristas—that don't require the skills or knowledge acquired when earning an undergraduate degree.

The trend toward increasing underemployment has many causes—some negative and some positive—including automation, the export of routine manufacturing jobs, an increase in the number of college graduates, and the growing opportunities for women in professions and positions once reserved for men. At the same time, the expectations of college-educated workers have also increased. Today, young graduates expect good jobs as their just reward for years of (increasingly expensive) higher education. Not only do these grads want high-paying jobs, they prefer work that is interesting and offers a chance for personal and career growth. Increasingly, many are not finding it.

The chronic underutilization of education, skills, and human capital engenders workplace frustration and low morale. That's why thoughtful employers must create conditions under which their employees are fully engaged in their work and, in turn, the company can capture greater value from those employees.

Effects of Underemployment

The effects of underemployment are similar to those of unemployment. First, both cause higher *poverty levels.* Without adequate income, families don't buy as much. That reduces consumer demand, slowing business growth. As a result, the nation's *Gross Domestic Product (GDP) is lower,* as is job growth.

If underemployment continues, workers *lose the ability to update their skills* with on-the-job training. They may not be able to return to their former field without training. *Some retrain for different fields,* while other downscale their lifestyle and accept long-term underemployment.

Younger people may find they never get a good start to their career. Forced to take jobs that are beneath their skills, they don't get on the *right career track.* They miss the mentoring needed to get increased responsibility that would update their skills. By the time the recession ends, they are competing with a new batch of graduates for entry-level positions in their fields.

In extreme cases, youth underemployment can lead to *civil unrest and violence*. For example, one fourth of all young people were unemployed in the Middle East, leading to the Arab Spring.

Psychological effect of underemployment/underemployment

Unemployment is commonly understood as an economic problem, and inquiries into its nature tend to come from that perspective. However, unemployment often exacts a toll that goes beyond economic concerns to psychological ones. Humans, after all, are not robots, and the loss of a job is not merely the loss of a paycheck but the loss of a routine, security, and connection to other people.

- *Individual and family consequences.*
  Job loss is associated with elevated rates of mental and physical health problems, increases in mortality rates, and detrimental changes in family relationships and in the psychological well-being of spouses and children. Compared to stably employed workers, those who have lost their jobs have *significantly poorer mental health, lower life satisfaction, less marital or family satisfaction, and poorer subjective physical health. Unemployment is associated with depression, anxiety, psychosomatic symptoms, low subjective well-being, and poor self-esteem.* Unemployed workers are twice as likely as their employed counterparts to experience psychological problems (Paul & Moser, 2009).

  Unemployment can contribute to *reduced life expectancy*. In a longitudinal study in which the employment, earnings, and work histories of high-seniority male workers were tracked during the 1970s and 1980s, mortality rates in the year after job displacement were 50 to 100 percent higher than would otherwise have been expected. The effect on mortality risk declined sharply over time, but even 20 years after these men had lost jobs, elevated risk of death was found among those who had lost jobs earlier, in comparison to the stably employed (Sullivan & von Wachter, 2009).

Low paying jobs typically offer minimal opportunities to utilize one's skills and come with a host of negative outcomes. *Underemployment is associated with decreased self-esteem, increased alcohol use, and elevated rates of depression, as well as low birthweight among babies born to underemployed women* (Dooley & Prause, 2004).

The stress of unemployment can lead to declines in the *well-being of spouses and to changes in family relationships and in outcomes for children.* Research dating back to the Great Depression found that men who experienced substantial financial loss became more irritable, tense, and explosive. Children often suffered as these fathers became more punitive and arbitrary in their parenting. Such paternal behavior, in turn, predicted temper tantrums, irritability, and negativism in children, especially boys, and moodiness, hypersensitivity, feelings of inadequacy and lowered aspirations in adolescent girls

Unemployment may even impact decisions about marriage and divorce. Unemployed or poor men are less likely to marry and more likely to divorce than men who are employed or who are more economically secure (McLoyd, 1990).

- *Community effects.*

The impact of unemployment extends beyond individuals and families to communities and neighborhoods. High unemployment and poverty go hand in hand, and the characteristics of *poor neighborhoods amplify the impact of* unemployment (Wilson, 1996).

Inadequate and low-quality housing, underfunded schools, few recreational activities, restricted access to services and public transportation, limited opportunities for employment - all characteristics of poor neighborhoods - contribute to the social, economic, and political exclusion of individuals and communities, making it more difficult for people to return to work.

Occupational networks are also impacted. Coworkers who have not lost their jobs may suffer from *anxiety that they, too, will soon be fired, and from a heavier work load, as they must now take on the work once done by their former colleagues.* Those who retain their jobs in the midst of downsizing may experience comparable physical and emotional effects to workers who lose their jobs.

Generally unemployment and underemployment have the following psychological and mental effect:

- Increase in stress level
- Depression
- Broken families
- General health issues
- Worries
- Anger
- Sadness

CHAPTER EIGHT: JOB SATISFACTION AND PERFORMANCE

Definition: Job satisfaction has been an important focal point for organisational and industrial psychology. In defining job satisfaction the reference is often made to Locke"s (1976) description of job satisfaction as a "pleasurable or positive emotional state resulting from the appraisal of one's job or job experiences". The appraisal involves various elements related to the job such as salary, working conditions, colleagues and boss, career prospects and, of course, the intrinsic aspects of the job itself (Arnold et al 1998 p. 204).

So, simply put, job satisfaction is connected to how our personal expectations of work are in congruence with the actual outcomes. And since job satisfaction is merely an employee's attitude towards his or job, previously discussed theories regarding attitudes are applicable to job satisfaction. Consequently job satisfaction can be seen as containing three components: an affective component, a cognitive component and a behavioral component (Jex 2002 p.116). While the affective component refers to a feeling about a job, the cognitive component represents a belief in regard to a job. Often these two aspects are related. The behavioral component is an indicator for behavioral intentions towards a job such as getting to work in time, working hard, etc.

Approaches to job satisfaction

In explaining job satisfaction and measuring the level of employees" satisfaction three different approaches have been developed.

The first approach turns its attention to the characteristics of the job and it is called the *"information processing model*. According to this model employees gather information about the job, the workplace and the organisation and cognitively assess these elements in order to determine the level of satisfaction.

The second approach suggests that the measurement of the level of job satisfaction is founded on „*social information"* –information based on past behaviour and what others at work think. It shifts its attention to the effects of the context and the consequences of past behaviour, rather than to individual predispositions and rational decision-making processes (Pennings 1986 p. 65).

Therefore job satisfaction is dependent on how others at work evaluate the workplace. This approach is called the *"social information processing model"* (Salancik and Pfeffer 1978).The third approach indicates that job satisfaction relies on the characteristics or the dis-positions of the employee. These dispositions can be based on experience or genetic heritage or on both.

In summary, job satisfaction can be seen as a function of:
• The features of a job,
• The view of others,
• The employee's personality

Job satisfaction and commitment

job satisfaction can affect a person's level of commitment to the organization, absenteeism, and job turnover rate. It can also affect performance levels, employee willingness to participate in problem-solving activities, and the amount of effort employees put in to perform activities outside their job description. When people are satisfied with the work they are doing, then their job feels less like work and is a more enjoyable experience. Those who are satisfied in their jobs usually do not find it difficult to get up and go to work.

Job satisfaction also reduces stress, which can affect job performance, mental well-being, and physical health. Stress can also affect decision-making possibly leading to unethical or nonstrategic choices. Satisfied employees, on the other hand, maintain a more positive and carefree perspective about work. This positive outlook often spreads to co-workers and can have a positive experience on everyone's performance. There are some indications that job satisfaction is directly tied to job performance; nonetheless, feeling less stressed can positively affect a person's behavior.

Methods for Increasing Job Satisfaction

To determine if employees are actually satisfied with the work they do, organizations frequently conduct surveys to measure employees' level of job satisfaction and to identify areas—on-boarding, job training, employee incentive programs, etc.—for improvement and job enrichment. Because job satisfaction varies for each individual, management teams employ several different strategies to help the majority of employees within an organization feel satisfied with their place in the company.

One proven way to enhance job satisfaction is rewarding employees based on performance and positive behavior. When employees go above and beyond their job description to complete a project or assist a colleague, their actions can be referred to as organizational citizenship behavior or OCB (Bommer, Miles, and Grover, 2003). Bommer, Miles, and Grover state:

Social-information processing is predicated on the notion that people form ideas based on information drawn from their immediate environment, and the behavior of co-workers is a very salient component of an employee's environment. Therefore, observing frequent citizenship episodes with in a workgroup are likely to lead to attitudes that such OCB is normal and appropriate. Consequently, the individual is likely to replicate this 'normal' behavior.

These positive changes in behavior show that people learn from their environments and that corporate culture plays a large part in creating job satisfaction. Managers are tasked with managing this positive culture and understanding how each employee is affected by cultural influences in the workplace. No two people are the same; this is where managers come into play. Managers must be insightful and observant, identifying what motivates high levels of job satisfaction in each individual and ensuring employees get what they need. In some ways, a manager's customers are their subordinates. Understanding this dynamic is an important component of the role of management.

JOB CONTENT AND ALIENATION

Concept and Meaning of Job Description and Contents of Job Description Statement

Job description is a functional description of the contents and contexts of the job. Job description narrates the various features and contents of a job. It is a written statement that identifies, describes and defines job's duties, responsibilities, working conditions etc. It is a document showing a brief summary of task requirements which explains the constitute elements of job in an organized way.

Job description discloses what an incumbent is supposed to do, how the task is to be done. The data to be included in the job description statement is usually determined by the job analyst to make the document more reliable and informative. Moreover, the information is, in turn, used to write a job specification statement showing minimum requirement of skill, knowledge and ability to perform a specific task.

Thus, job description is the listing of job tasks, duties and responsibilities which depicts a brief summary of the job in terms of nature and types.

Contents of Job Description Statement

The job description statement contains the following contents:

1. Job Title

It explains the title of the job. It means, what the particular job is all about is identified under this content.

2. Job Location

It refers to the name of the department where the job under consideration exists in the organization.

3. Job Summary

Job summary tells about a brief history of job. It is a short paragraph which explains the tasks and activities to be performed by an incumbent. It is a statement which explains what the job entails.

4. Duties

Duties refer to the task performed by an employee. It is necessary to mention the task of the employee because it helps him to estimate the percentage of time that is devoted to the performance.

5. Machines, Tools and Equipment

The machines, tools and equipment used by an incumbent for the performance of tasks are included under this head.

6. Materials and Form Used

It includes all input requirements and the method of application in the production process.

7. Working Environment

The working environment is concerned with the actual work place. It defines working condition in terms of heat, light, noise level etc.

8. Job Hazards

Job hazards are obstacles and obstructions that may arise during actual performance of the task.

Concept and Meaning of Job Specification and Contents of Job Specification Statement

Job specification is a document or statement which spells out the minimum levels of qualification, skills, physical and other abilities, experience, judgement and attributes required to perform the efficiently and effectively. Job specification is prepared along with job description statement to explain the minimum acceptable human qualities necessary to perform the task effectively. It specifies the physical, psychological, personal, social and behavioral characteristics of each job-holder.

The job specification statement is an important tool in the selection process because it specifies the individual abilities, skills and knowledge of performing tasks. It keeps the selector's attentions on the list of qualifications necessary for an incumbent to perform the job. Finally, it allows him/her to determine whether candidates are qualified.

Therefore, a job specification is the listing of minimum levels of qualification, skills and abilities that an incumbent must possess in order to perform the required task properly. An individual possessing the minimum qualities specified in a job specification statement can perform the job more effectively than individual lacking them.

Contents of Job Specification Statement
1. Required Education
Required level of education for each post that an incumbent is supposed to hold is listed in job specification statement. It also helps to determine the level or category of job in terms of rank.

2. Health and Physical Fitness
Physical fitness and health is a crucial aspect of good performance. Hence, body structure, physical ability and other aspects of health and fitness is a must in order to perform well in the organization.

3. Appearance
Appearance refers to an outlook of an employee, which must be attractive and good looking. The cleanliness and neatness of an individual shows his/her appearance. Hence, job specification statement defines the employee's appearance.

4. Mental and Other Abilities
The employee must be mentally fit to perform the desired task. If not, the problems may arise at the work floor. Mental fitness is associated with the ability of decision making, managing emotions and sorrows, dealing with different kinds of people etc.

5. Experience

Under it, the required level of experience in doing a particular task is explained, if necessary. An experienced employee will be preferable in comparison to the fresh candidate.

ALIENATION

The term 'alienation' originates from the work of Karl Marx on the effects on workers of the capitalist labour process and is well described in a number of studies (Bottomore and Rubel, 1961; Corlett, 1988; Fox,1974; Hyman,1975; ,1968; Taylor,1967). According to Marx, alienation is a condition in which the individual becomes isolated and cut off from the product of his or her work, having given up the desire for self-expression and control over his or her own fate at work. The individual enacts a role estranged from the kind of life of which the individual is capable. The genesis of this condition can be traced to changes external to the individual arising out of the industrialization process, with the creation of large factories characterized by organizational hierarchies, job specialization, and work supervision reliant on formal authority, and a shift in life focus away from the home and community to the organization

Human resource management View:

Alienation is a sense of estrangement felt by employees, reflected in their lack of warmth towards the organization and in believing that their job/work is not meaningful to other aspects of their lives. Alienation is caused commonly by factors such as a lack of involvement in even basic decision making, lack of human contact, little hope for betterment, and a feeling of powerlessness.

When workers are disengaged, retention shouldn't be a company's only concern — productivity and customer service levels also suffer. There are many factors that contribute to strong employee engagement — chief among them are the ability of staff to reach professional goals and understand how they contribute to the organization's big-picture objectives."

How employees are alienated and how to address it

- **Keeping them in the dark.**

Instead: Whenever feasible, employers should give their staff updates on the company's financial performance and long- and short-term goals, and explain what this information means for them and their jobs. Sharing this will help them feel connected to the organization.

- **Not asking for their input.**

Instead: Actively seek feedback from team members. Managers and company leaders should maintain an open-door policy, and an open mind, so that it's easy for individuals to approach them. They should also reach out to those who may be uncomfortable voicing their thoughts to ensure their ideas are heard.

- **Keeping them boxed in.**

Instead: Businesses should encourage staff members to take on new responsibilities and projects. By giving workers a chance to try new things, they'll demonstrate their confidence in them and help them build new skills.

- **Ignoring their goals.**

Instead: It's crucial for employees to set career goals so they feel they're working toward something and can see that the company supports their professional aspirations. Employers should talk to their staff about their ambitions and work with them on plans for meeting those objectives.

- **Working them too hard.**

Instead: Leaders need to remind workers to take regular breaks to recharge, and set a good example by doing so themselves. When the team seems particularly stressed, organize a

TRAINING AND LEARNING AT WORK

Most of the knowledge and skills anyone possesses are a result of the things they have learned during work and on the job. Workplace learning is mainly informal, taking place through work-related actions, meaning that people learn more from each other and during the process of finding solutions for their day-to-day problems at the workplace. In addition, work-related learning also includes self-directed learning, networking, coaching and mentoring, contributing to the development of the employee and of the organisation as a whole.

Learning at work is a great way to fit learning into your life, and could help improve your career prospects. Building essential skills into a workplace is simply good business. Incorporating essential skills into your workplace process and practices allows you to tap into your largest asset, develop the widest range of talent, and better position your organization to avoid skills gaps and shortages. How?

- Learning about essential skills helps you better understand and respond to workplace challenges
- Investing in essential skills and workplace learning improves job success and training outcomes for you and your employees and access to services and products for your clients and customers
- Promoting learning in the workplace can help your employees gain the skills to adapt and grow into new and needed skill areas
- Developing workplace learning practices increases employees' job satisfaction and engagement satisfaction, reduces turnover and saves money. All of which ensure positive results for businesses and for individuals.

By promoting workplace learning and essential skills, you contribute to your corporate image. Share your success and build on it. As an employer, report on how learning in the workplace and essential skills development have contributed to your workplace. Communicate your good news. Celebrate your success with stories in company newsletters, press releases to community or trade publications, or reports to shareholders. Fostering learning in the workplace creates a win-win situation for you, your workforce and your customers.

For you as an employer, focusing on learning is an efficient and highly effective way to:

- Increase employee retention and loyalty
- Promote employees to higher and better paying positions
- Provide improved customer service

- Improve overall morale and workplace relationships
- Interest employees in further learning and training
- Improve your workplace communication strategies
- Develop a culture of learning at work

For your employees, it is a way to:

- Increase their self-esteem and feel valued
- Increase their interest in ongoing learning and training
- Learn additional skills that apply to work, family and community life
- Enhance their language and essential skills
- Feel more comfortable in their present jobs
- Apply for better paying jobs
- Get promoted in their workplace
- Get involved in and be successful in future learning opportunities

Overall outcomes of workplace learning for employers

Common results reported by employers with respect to their employees and overall workplace include:

- Greater confidence and self-esteem on the part of employees
- Better success in different kinds of job-related training
- More independence and skills for using technology
- Increased ability to work independently
- Improved productivity
- Better teamwork
- Greater adaptability to workplace change
- Better morale at the workplace
- Improved health and safety
- Increased decision making and participation at work
- Greater participation in learning and training opportunities

Overall outcomes for employees

Employees who have participated in workplace learning report the following outcomes:

- Greater confidence and self-esteem
- Improved reading, writing and speaking skills
- Better ability to complete work tasks especially those involving paperwork and technology
- Improved relationships with co-workers
- Greater interest in further training and education.

Continuous learning

On a personal level, *continuous learning* is about the constant expansion of skills and skill-sets through learning and increasing knowledge. As life changes the need to adapt both professionally and personally is as real as the changes themselves.

On a professional level, continuous learning is about further expanding our skill-set in response to a changing environment and new developments. This is very important because we are called to respond to changes daily; for example, the introduction of computers in the workplace created a need for people to train on computers to complete tasks more efficiently. On a personal level, the introduction of computers made us rethink how we communicate with people and allowed us to keep in touch with people across the globe with just the click of a button.

Continuous learning for Individuals and Groups

On an individual level, continuous learning is defined by the practices the individual carries out daily in order to continue increasing knowledge. For example:

- Asking for help when something is not understood
- Observing more experienced employees at work
- Trying new ways of doing things and exploring alternative methods
- Practicing what has been learnt already

- Finding ways to improve such as taking up training programs or online seminars outside of work

In the organization, continuous learning has to do with shaping a team to adapt to changes in the business environment. This is very important because the ever-changing economic climate demands that any team be up to date with the latest knowledge and also be flexible and easily adaptable to any changes that may be required.

Business Sustainability and Continuous Learning

Embracing a culture of "investing in people" has played a major role in companies training their employees rather than hiring new people which can be much more costly on different levels. Most companies nowadays want to invest in retaining their talent - and developing that pool of talent - so they keep employees well trained and up-to-date so that they can respond to the company's ever-changing needs. This also develops a sense of trust and keeps employees engaged and interested since new skills are constantly added to their 'arsenal'. Apart from saving money, continuous learning is a means for a company to show its employees they are worth investing in

CHAPTER NINE: WORK LEISURE AND RETIREMENT

Community views on retirement are polarized. Some see it as an opportunity to escape work obligations and pursue their own passions. Others view the transition as a loss of status, social connectedness, and financial security.

The view that retirement has a negative effect on mental health is consistent with decades of evidence about the impacts of job loss among young and middle-aged people. And the transition to retirement is certainly a major milestone and lifestyle change, given the central roles work and career play in most people's lives.

Studies comparing the mental health of retirees with that of working older adults have shown that retirees (particularly men) tend to have greater levels of depression and anxiety than their working peers.

But longitudinal studies that track the mental health of people moving from work to retirement offers little proof that this transition has a significant detrimental impact on the mental health of most people. Indeed, it seems more likely that the poor mental health observed among many retirees precedes and perhaps has *driven* their workforce exit.

The reasons for retirement, whether people left work gradually or continue to work in some capacity during retirement, and the age at which people leave work have all been shown to affect mental health among retirees.

Not surprisingly, involuntary or unexpected job loss in later life is the form of retirement that has been most consistently linked to increased depression. On the other hand, part or gradual retirement (rather than full departure from the workforce) may ease the stress associated with leaving the workforce. Retirement has the most positive psychological effects for people with strong social supports.

We are all familiar with the popular image of early retirement being a luxury enjoyed by financially secure individuals who lead full and satisfied lives. However, contrary to this widely held idea research shows that early retirees tend to have much poorer mental health than their working peers and older retirees.

Again, this may in part reflect the reasons for their early workforce exit, such as existing health concerns. But these studies also suggest that poor mental health may stem from being out of the workforce at an age when most of one's peers are still working.

Workplace conditions can also impact upon people's decisions to stay at work. Older people with stressful jobs or jobs that offer little security or autonomy have poor mental health and tend to retire early. Improving conditions at work may encourage better mental health and longer workforce engagement for older adults.

Once retired, who does best?

Retirement has the strongest positive psychological effect on people with solid social supports. Older adults who are engaged in their communities and spend more time with family and friends have better mental health than others. And this is particularly true for retirees, as community participation has added meaning and importance to one's mental health once paid work has finished.

Countries are constantly looking for ways to maintain the health – both mental and physical – of older adults and encourage their continued participation in the workforce. Knowing the risk factors for mental health problems as a result of workforce exit in later life is key to these goals.

The questions most people think about before retirement are "How much money will I need?" and "Am I saving enough?" But while financial security is certainly critical, people need to amass more than money for a successful retirement, experts say. They need to stockpile their emotional reserves, as well.

Too few people consider the psychological adjustments that accompany this life stage, which can include coping with the loss of your career identity, replacing support networks you had through work, spending more time than ever before with your spouse and finding new and engaging ways to stay active.

Some retirees ease smoothly into retirement, spending more time with hobbies or family and friends. But others, research finds, experience anxiety, depression and debilitating feelings of loss. People can go through hell when they retire and they will never say a word about it, often because they are embarrassed. The cultural norm for retirement is that you are living the good life.

Research by psychologists and others has found that working or volunteering during retirement can help stave off depression, as well as dementia and hypertension. But other evidence suggests that such activities aren't the key to everyone's well-being. Only those people who are truly engaged in their post-retirement activities reap the psychological benefits. That's why people need to invest as much if not more time in their social or psychological portfolio planning before retirement, to figure out what makes them happy. Retirement is not like jumping off a diving board, it's a process and it takes time," she says. There's a lot of work people can be doing leading up to retirement to prepare for it.

Working toward well-being

Soon-to-be retirees should consider whether or not to continue to work in some capacity. Many people take on new jobs after retiring from their primary careers with part-time work, a temporary job or self. While working has obvious financial perks, it may also offer health and mental health benefits. A 2009 study led by Mo Wang, PhD, of the University of Florida, found that people who pursued post-retirement bridge employment in their previous fields reported better mental and physical health than those who retired fully (*Journal of Occupational Health Psychology*). The Working in Retirement report found that employed retirees report levels of health, well-being and life satisfaction on par with those who have not yet retired — despite age differences. The report also found that working retirees tend to rate their workplaces more positively than those not yet retired.

The 6 Stages of Retirement

Most major life-changing events, such as marriage or divorce, involve an ongoing process of emotional adjustment. Retirement is no exception. Marriage, divorce and other family-related issues have been the focus of decades of research and analysis by both clinical therapists and religious institutions.

Unfortunately, the emotional and psychological frontier of retirement has remained virtually unexplored until recently. However, while research on this subject has barely begun, it is clear that the psychological process of retirement process follows a pattern similar in nature to the emotional phases accompanying other areas of transition. Read on to discover the six stages of retirement and what you can do to prepare for this important life transition.

Retirees must face what is essentially the last transition in their lives. The first transition comes when we leave the security of home to begin our school life in kindergarten, and after school we have the rest of the day to ourselves. Another major transition comes when we join the working world. Now we work all week but still have the weekend to ourselves. Then finally comes retirement, a time when careers are over and the work is done. Retirees have the rest of their *lives* to themselves. The transition into retirement can be broken down into six main phases. Let's take a closer look at each of these phases.

1. Pre-retirement - Planning Time

During the working years, retirement can appear to be both an oncoming burden and a distant paradise. Workers know that this stage of their lives is coming, and do everything they can to save for it, but often give little thought to what they will actually *do* once they reach the goal - the current demands that are placed upon them leave them little time to ponder this issue. Many people face retirement like a running back on the football field who dodges or plows through one defender after another until reaching the end zone. It's hard for many workers to think seriously about what their lives will be like in 20 or 30 years when they are trying to stay on top of their mortgage, put their kids through college and have a little fun in the meantime. They want to reach the end zone, but other issues will tackle them long before then if they don't take immediate action.

2. The Big Day - Smiles, Handshakes, Farewells

By far the shortest stage in the retirement process is the actual cessation of employment itself. This is often marked by some sort of dinner, party or other celebration, and has become a rite of passage for many, especially for those with distinguished careers. In some respects, this event is comparable to the ceremony that marks the beginning of a marriage.

3. Honeymoon Phase - I'm Free!

Of course, honeymoons follow more than just weddings. Once the retirement celebrations are over, a period often follows where retirees get to do all the things that they wanted to do once they stopped working, such as travel, indulge in hobbies, visit relatives and so forth. This phase has no set time frame and will vary depending upon how much honeymoon activity the retiree has planned.

4. Disenchantment - So this is it?

This phase parallels the stage in marriage when the emotional high of the wedding has worn off and the couple now has to get down to the business of building a working relationship together. After looking forward to this stage for so long, many retirees must deal with a feeling of letdown, similar to that of newlyweds who must get down the the business of living once the honeymoon is over. Retirement isn't a permanent vacation after all; it also can bring lowliness, boredom, feelings of uselessness and disillusionment.

5. Reorientation - Building a New Identity

Fortunately, the letdown phase of retirement doesn't last forever. Just as married couples eventually learn how to live together, retirees begin to familiarize themselves with the landscape of their new circumstances and navigate their lives accordingly. This is easily the most difficult stage in the emotional retirement process and will take both time and conscious effort to accomplish. Perhaps the most difficult aspects of this stage to manage are the inevitable self-examination questions that must be answered once again, such as "Who am I, now?", "What is my purpose at this point?" and "Am I still useful in some capacity?" New - and satisfying - answers to these questions must be found if the retiree is to feel a sense of closure from his or her working days. But many retirees cannot achieve this and never truly escape this stage - make sure you do!

6. Routine - Moving On

Finally, a new daily schedule is created, new marital ground rules for time together versus time alone are established, and a new identity has been at least partially created. Eventually, the new landscape becomes familiar territory, and retirees can enjoy the last phase of their lives with a new sense of purpose.

Conclusion

Life planning is an important key to successful retirement. Workers that have given serious time and thought to what they will do after they retire will generally experience a smoother transition than those who haven't. Dreams and goals that cannot be achieved with a single trip or project may translate into long-term part-time employment or volunteer work. But it is never too soon to begin mapping out the course of the rest of your life. As with all emotional processes that can be broken down into separate phases, it is not necessary to completely achieve one phase before beginning another (except, of course, for the actual cessation of employment). But virtually all retirees will experience some form of this process after they stop working. Their ability to navigate these uncharted waters will ultimately determine how they live the last phase of their lives

Tips for Adjusting to Retirement

When your life is dominated by the daily grind, the idea of one day retiring and simply doing nothing may seem fantastic. However, retirement takes its toll not only financially but also emotionally. Even if it isn't part of your plans for the near future, the sooner you start preparing for retirement, the easier it will be to adjust to this huge life change when the time comes

1. Get Your Savings in Order

It's never too early to start saving for retirement but the closer you get to retirement age, the more important it is to put away enough money for when you don't get that regular paycheque anymore.

2. Downsize Your Home

Another way to boost your savings, according to All Women's Talk, is to find a smaller, cheaper home. After all, will you really need those four bedrooms once the kids have left the nest?

3. Budget

When you don't have a regular income anymore, you'll have to learn to get by with the money that you do have. How Stuff Works suggests that you draw up a budget and then stick to it.

4. Don't Build Your Entire Identity around Your Job

A common emotional pitfall for retirees, according to Everyday Health, is the loss of identity after a lifetime of calling yourself a doctor, a writer, a computer analyst or whatever your job has been. Try building your identity around other aspects of your life, such as your hobbies or your likes and dislikes.

5. Have Friends Outside of Work

When you retire, your social circle may suddenly shrink as you lose your friends from work. To avoid this, start building friendships with people other than your co-workers

6. Stay Socially Connected

Forbes also says that it's important to stay socially connected once you've retired. Make new friends or reconnect with old ones so that you don't build your social life only around your family.

7. Find Ways to Reduce Stress

Retirement can be very stressful and Everyday Health suggests that you look into meditation, exercise, therapy or other practices that can reduce stress. Getting into these habits now will also help you cope with life pre-retirement

8. Stay Active

How Stuff Works says that you need to stay active after retirement because just sitting around the house will be bad for you, both physically and mentally

9. Set Goals

According to Forbes, it will be easier to adjust to retirement if you set goals, from little ones like taking a shower and dressing in something other than your PJs to bigger ones, like looking for a volunteer jo

10. Build a New Routine

Everyday Health suggests that you build a new daily routine. For example, walk the dog or have a regular coffee date with a friend

11. Find Your New Path

Think about what you want to do with all that newfound free time. Maybe you want to keep doing something similar to the job you've had but, as Everyday Health says, doing something completely different is a great way to make new friends and challenge yourself

12. Build Skills You Can Use Post-Retirement

According to How Stuff Works, it's a good idea to keep working in some capacity after retirement. So, start building skills that you can use in a part-time or freelance capacity, or that can help you start and run your own business.

13. Share Your Skills

A common side effect of retirement is the feeling of not being useful anymore. How Stuff Works suggests that you find ways of sharing your skills and experience, for instance by teaching or mentoring.

14. Take up New Hobbies

All Women's Talk suggests that you take up new hobbies to help you stay active, get out in the world and stimulate your mind

15. Go Back to School

A great way to keep your mind stimulated is to go back to school and take classes in a field that you're interested in, rather than classes that will help advance your career. How Stuff Works says that you can attend free or very affordable audit classes at many institutions, where you don't take exams or earn a qualification

16. Volunteer

By volunteering, you get to share your skills, learn new ones, stick to a routine, stay active and meet new people. You'll also feel useful and, as How Stuff Works says, it may help you live longer

17. Take up a Cause

How Stuff Works points out that there are many ways to get involved in causes that you care about, from joining grassroots organizations to volunteering at the polls on election day

18. Work on Your Relationship

As All Women's Talk points out, retirement means that you'll be spending more time with your partner than what either of you is used to. Work on strengthening your relationship so that it will weather the inevitable storms

19. Set Boundaries

According to All Women's Talk, a common problem for retirees is that people may see you as a free childcare service. You'll need to set boundaries and make it clear how much of your time you're willing to give to others.

20. Travel

Once you've retired, you finally have the time and money to go see the world, and as How Stuff Works points out, you'll also be able to make use of the many discounts for senior citizens. Travelling will help you stay active, and you can even make a difference in some exotic location by doing volunteer work

CHAPTER TEN: PSYCHOLOGICAL NEGOTIATION

5 Psychological Negotiation Methods That Allowed Me to Close Huge Deals

1. Absolute Integrity

The squeaky clean sound of this qualification could be a little off putting. Let me explain.

Integrity, when viewed from a psychological perspective, is the attribute of consistency. A person who is viewed by others as possessing integrity will reflect consistent behavior across a variety of life situations.

When you sit down to negotiate with people whom you have not yet met personally, they will know you by your reputation. Thus, they have some preconceived notion of how you're going to act and talk.

How did they learn about your reputation? They probably did a few online searches. They scoped out your LinkedIn profile, read your "about" page on the company website, and viewed a blog post you wrote. Now, they know a little bit about you.

They will interpret your behavior in the meeting based on the perception they formed of you.

Your reputation must possess integrity. There is no other way for your negotiators to see your integrity other than to identify consistency between your reputation and your behavior. Remember, integrity is about consistency.

Their only benchmark for consistency is what they think they know about you from your online reputation. Does your reputation make you look greedy? Do you brag about your lifestyle? Does your published content reflect balance and fairness?

In today's world, you can't afford to neglect your online reputation. It is crucial to your success in business.

If you lack integrity in your negotiations, you're off to a disadvantaged start. During the entire negotiation process, you will be working to build integrity or to overcome a poor online reputation.

2. Mirroring

During the 1990s, Dr. Giacomo Rizzolatti at the University of Parma made an astonishing discovery. While evaluating the behavior and neurology of macaque monkeys, he realized that the primate's innate sense of imitation was linked to specific brain neurons.

When one monkey reached for an object, a monkey who observed that monkey would experience activation in the same part of the brain. It is such a powerful mental phenomena that the neurons are activated simply through observation.

Mirror neurons are now a heavily researched and verified aspect of neuroscience and psychology. The concept is simple, and can be described like this: Monkey see. Monkey do.

When you see someone smile, frown, cry, stand, sit, walk, bow, hunch, leap, or any other motor movement, neurons in your brain start to do the same thing. Your mental mimicry may even result in the same action.

If someone smiles at you, you are more likely to smile back. Why? You may tell yourself that it is because you're trying to be polite. Actually, your brain primed your body for smiling the instant you saw that person's face break into a smile.

How does this apply to the negotiation table? Mirroring another person's actions develops an underlying sense of empathy between the two people.

If the person across the table from you folds their arms over their chest, you might, a few moments later, do the same thing. If, on the other hand, one person at the table leans forward with her elbows on the table others may start to do the same after a few minutes.

If you want to be perceived as responsive, engaging, empathetic, or understanding, traits that may improve your persuasion potential, then you should make a conscious effort to mirror the actions, facial expressions, and attitudes of the other party.

3. Cross your arms to indicate inflexibility.

Body language can be just as powerful as verbal language in a negotiation.

One of the most powerful moves is folding one's arms. It's a power move, and in some situations, you shouldn't do it. Why not? Because it "signals defensiveness and resistance" according to a Forbes piece on body language.

If your intent in the negotiation is to say "no" to a proposal then go ahead and cross your arms. If you've given them your final number or a deal breaker line item, cross your arms.

You must be aware that crossing your arms says something definitive and consequential.

4. Spread your arms to indicate openness.

Most postures have some level of meaning, although you don't want to take it too far.

If your intent is to indicate openness to negotiation, then spread your arms, or at least leave them at your side. An open mentality is reflected in an open physical posture.

5. Dress to impress.

It's cliché to advise "dress to impress." Worn-out as it sounds, there is powerful psychology behind one's appearance.

First, and most forgotten, is that dressing up affects your mind. The better you feel about your appearance, the better you act. You are more likely to act in a confident, impressive, and powerful way.

Equally important is the impression it makes on the other person. She perceives you as someone who exhibits good taste, a concern for self, a concern for others, and overall competence in life.

Dressing nicely can change the entire tenor and outcome of the negotiation process. "Dress the message."

CHAPTER ELEVEN: CONCLUSION

Each of these tactics requires you to say nothing. Each of the tactics are formed or performed in the mind, and their impact is subtle and unstated.

That is precisely why they are so effective. A negotiation process is about changing one's mind, about minds connecting in agreement. It is important to understand how the mind functions in order to improve your chances of success.

What psychological knowledge has made you a successful negotiator?

Essential Negotiation Strategies

1. You Can Negotiate Anything

The first thing you should know about negotiating is that everything is fair game, not just cars and houses. At stores, we tend to look at price tags and presume that the offer is final. It rarely ever is. At the very minimum, you should always ask the clerk if they have any coupons available or if any other discounts apply.

2. Ask to Speak With a Manager or Owner

Most sales clerks don't really care if you make a purchase or not. They're getting paid minimum wage, and your purchases won't put any more money in their pocket. So the second step is to find the person at the store who will directly benefit from the sale. Ideally, you will want to speak with the owner of a small store, but that is impossible with most bigger retailers.

In those cases, look for the manager, whose compensation is most often tied to store sales and customer satisfaction. Ask him if they will offer a discount if you purchase more than one of the item, or if you're a regular customer, ask for a small percentage off retail as a loyalty reward. The key is to let them know that the sale is dependent on their response, otherwise they have no incentive.

3. Keep a Poker Face

If you see an item you want and exclaim loudly that it's perfect and that you've been seeking it for all of your life, there is little incentive for the other party to negotiate. Always keep your cool and don't display any unusual interest in the item. When asked, limit your enthusiasm while unfavorably comparing it to other products. Then suggest that you might still be interested for the right price.

The strength of your negotiating position relies on your actual alternatives to this deal. As a buyer, you should never fixate on a single product; always shop around and keep your options open. As a seller, you should always be prepared to seek more potential buyers.

4. Don't Make the First Offer and Don't Negotiate with Yourself

Whether you are buying or selling, you never want to make the first offer. Why? Because the other party may offer a price that is a much better deal than what you initially had in mind. If you're buying, consider the starting point to be the list price, but make it clear that the price is too high. From there, ask the seller if there is any flexibility and force the seller to offer you a lower price. It is only at that point you should make your first offer.

But once you have made your offer, do not volunteer another price unless and until the other party has responded with a counteroffer. Expect the negotiations to be a back-and-forth process, but remain confident throughout.

5. Bundle

A great way to augment your negotiation over price is to include other items. When you reach an impasse in your negotiations, an offer to purchase multiple quantities of the item or additional items might trigger flexibility on the part of the seller.

The seller may be willing to lose a customer if it's a single item. But when a seller has the opportunity to make a much larger transaction, there is a much greater likelihood he will be amenable to a lower price.

Likewise, as a seller you can negotiate the buyer to a higher price by throwing in an extra item. If you're selling your house, for instance, and you have brand new porch furniture that fits the deck perfectly, offer to include it in the price you want as an incentive to the buyer.

6. Barter

Do you have any items that might be of interest to the seller? Could you offer some services that would be of value to the seller? Consider making a trade to eliminate or significantly offset the need for actual dollars in a transaction. The idea is to use creativity in order to reach a deal that might otherwise not come to fruition. As a starting point, you can find many bartering websites online.

7. Use Silence and Time as a Tactic

Never respond too quickly to an offer. Pausing or even suspending negotiations can convey that you're not desperate to close the deal and that you have other options. Silence can force a surprising amount of pressure on the other party as well.

8. Be Willing to Walk Away

Even if it's the car, television, or house of your dreams, if the seller won't come down to the maximum price you have set for your budget, force yourself to walk out of the store or away from the deal. This strong stance more often than not will get you the price you're looking for, as the seller doesn't want to lose the sale. In flea markets and overseas, for example, I often get my best price only as I am literally walking away from the shop.

9. Keep It Light

You never want to let negotiations become too tense. Always feel free to smile and inject some humor in the conversation. Lightening up the mood can ingratiate you with your opponent while also conveying your negotiating strength. If you do not appear to be taking the negotiation extremely seriously, your opponent may conclude that you are ready to move on if you don't get the price you want.

10. Use Written Communication If Possible

In foreign markets, it's common to negotiate in writing on a pad using just numbers. This solves language barriers while producing a record of the negotiations. Furthermore, it's just easier to communicate non-verbally when negotiating back and forth. Non-verbal communication strips away all of cues that one's body language and tone of voice can give away – which is why most real estate deals are made through realtors and in writing.

Outside of foreign markets, you will find it easier to negotiate back and forth over email or even through an online chat for customer service. Email is a great medium for negotiating the purchase or sale of a car or other household goods on websites like Craigslist. Email also provides you with the time to analyze the situation and make an educated, non-panicked counteroffer.

11. Practice

The only way to become an expert negotiator is to practice a lot. In the United States, the closest things we have to traditional markets are flea markets and garage sales. Spending a day or two bickering over t-shirts or used furniture will improve your negotiating skills and give you the confidence that will be valuable when you purchase a car or a house. It's also a great idea to practice in foreign countries, where bargaining is much more widely accepted and even expected.

Six Surprising Negotiation Tactics That Get You the Best Deal

Here are the recommended best practices from Grant and Galinsky. How do yours compare?

1. Share information.

We often approach negotiation being very guarded and wary of showing our cards. Yet, while we believe this is a smart approach, it has a negative impact on our outcomes and inhibits trust. As Grant points out, people tend to be matchers and "follow the norm of reciprocity, responding in kind to how we treat them." If we want to be trusted, we must first offer it.

Studies have shown that revealing some information, even when it's unrelated to the negotiation, increases the outcome. You don't have to put all of your cards on the table at the outset. Simply putting something of yourself out there – your hobbies, personal concerns, or hopes – can set a positive tone that's conducive to gaining agreement.

2. Rank orders your priorities.

Typically when we negotiate, we know what our key issues are, and we sequence them. For example, if we're trying to close a new client, we might say that the price is most important, and if we don't agree, there's no use to continue.

Grant recommends another approach called rank ordering. His research shows that you are able to achieve better outcomes by ranking and leaving all the issues on the table and being transparent about it. That way both parties can compare their rankings and determine what the full set of options really is.

In the above example, perhaps you could make trade-offs in scope or travel requirements if the client can't get to your price.

3. Go in knowing your target price and your walkaway terms.

Galinsky calls your walkaway price (or terms) your *reservation price*. Your *target price* is what you're hoping for. Often we go into negotiations with one or the other – or let our partner start the bidding. This puts us at a huge disadvantage.

It's critical to do the research ahead of time here. You need your research to be based on firm data, as not only will it provide more confidence and power to you, but it also reduces the chance that you'll throw something crazy out there. By knowing your own range, it will help you make better decisions in the moment, and be clear about your limits.

4. Make the first offer.

This is one piece of advice that clearly defies conventional wisdom. In negotiations, information is often equated with power. We believe it's best to extract as much as possible from the other person before tipping our own hand.

Grant and Galinsky both agree that the research is clear on this point: people who make first offers get better terms that are closer to their target price. The reason is the psychological principle of anchoring. Whatever the first number is on the table, both parties begin to work around it. It sets the stage.

Often we are reluctant to go first because we may be way off, and disengage the other party. But Galinksy notes that this does not play out in the research. He said that most people make first offers that aren't aggressive enough.

There's a reason we have the adage, "you get what you pay for." Higher prices make the buyer focus on the positives, while lower ones invite focus on the downsides. In other words, we find data that supports this anchor. (Consider real estate: a high-priced home makes us look at all the desirable qualities, while a below-market offering brings up a bad location or needed repairs.)

Galinsky says that ideally the best first offer is one that's just outside your partner's reservation price, but not so far that they have sticker shock.

5. Don't counter too low.

If you aren't able to make the first offer, then you need to also protect yourself against the anchoring effect. Caution: most people go too low, too quickly. Your counter should be based on the same information you would have used if you'd made the first offer, Galinsky says.

You may also want to consider re-anchoring, as Grant puts it. Let the other person know that their offer is way off, and go back in with a new reset. It also may be helpful to call out what you're observing to redirect the conversation, i.e. you may be trying to test my thinking with that first offer, but here's more of what I had in mind.

6. Counter offers make both parties more satisfied.

Every buyer wants to feel that they got a good deal; every seller wants to feel as if they drove a hard bargain. Parties are most satisfied on both fronts if there was some back and forth. This may come as a surprise if you're someone who abhors negotiation.

Galinsky even advises that you shouldn't take the first offer, even if it meets your needs. By going back and asking for concessions you can ensure that you got the best deal, and increase your partner's satisfaction as well. More satisfied partners are more likely to work harder and be more committed to the end result, which is the ideal outcome from the start.